Bold, intelligent, and convicting. Even as culture rewards our masks, *Veneer* urges us to rip them off. The life we ought to live is identified on these pages. Read only if you are ready to shed your façade.

— Gabe Lyons, founder of Q and author of *The Next Christians*

Our culture wants an "app for happiness," and the church too often imitates that "app culture." *Veneer* contains the best exposure of our "Celebrity Me!" culture I've seen, and once Willard and Locy have peeled back the veneer, they take us on a journey into knowing God. A must-read for parents and leaders. I'll be putting copies of this into the hands of my students.

— Scot McKnight, author of *One.Life: Jesus Calls, We Follow*

When I put down this book, I felt seen, heard, and not crazy. That's about the highest compliment I can give. *Veneer* asked me to look at the truth about myself — consumerism, celebrity gawking, the temptation to give people a curated and manufactured Facebook profile version of myself. And then it reminded me of a better way: deep relationships, intimacy, face-to-face connections, honesty even when it's ugly. It reminded me how I want to live.

— Shauna Niequist, author of *Bittersweet*

The more I read *Veneer*, the more I wanted to keep reading. The writing is refreshingly winsome and artful. Willard and Locy draw from masters, past and present, to offer an incisive cultural theology that drives us toward the knowledge and magnificence of God as the antidote to the superficial cloak of self-love and image management so common in today's world. Compelling, fascinating, challenging — *Veneer* gives you permission to be you.

— Chip Ingram, author and president of Living on the Edge

With artful brilliance, Locy and Willard expose the emptiness of our consumer-driven society and illuminate the veneer in all of us. With compelling illustrations and daring reflection, you will be invited to live an authentic life. Get ready to be changed.

— Phileena Heuertz, author of *Pilgrimage of a Soul: Contemplative Spirituality for the Active Life*

In a time when so many Christian books offer a lot of sizzle and not much steak, it's satisfying to find one that defies the trend. Willard and Locy artfully diagnose the shallowness of our culture and call those belonging to Christ into deeper waters. Rather than emulating our society to win wider approval, they encourage us back to Scripture and a more profound communion with God.

— Skye Jethani, senior editor of *Leadership*

In a culture commonly driven by consumption, many long for a deeper level of connection that is missing in our busy, lonely lives. Willard and Locy begin to address the questions you've only dared to ask in the quietness of your soul. This book will help in the too-often futile search for significance, the significance that shallow success, cheap celebrity, and surface-level acquaintanceships could never provide. *Veneer* is timely and powerful, a deeply compelling work that will surely resonate with this generation.

— Kevin Palau, president of Luis Palau Association

Veneer is an insightful book for the times that we live in. Willard and Locy have pulled back the layers as to why the church fails to thrive, and the importance of going deep in a surface world. A compelling, informative, and timely read.

— Jon Tyson, lead pastor of Trinity Grace New York City

Willard and Locy take a hard look at our society and then provide a gentle and persuasive nudge into a new perspective. A pleasure to read, *Veneer* will challenge us all.

— Darren Whitehead, teaching pastor at Willow Creek

The message of *Veneer* is one that every leader needs to hear and adopt. Willard and Locy have provided a much needed "reset" on how we should all think, live, and be.

— Brad Lomenick, director of Catalyst

VENEER

LIVING DEEPLY IN A SURFACE SOCIETY

Timothy D. Willard and R. Jason Locy

ZONDERVAN.com/
AUTHORTRACKER
follow your favorite authors

ZONDERVAN

Veneer

Copyright © 2011 by R. Jason Locy and Timothy Willard

This title is also available as a Zondervan ebook. Visit www.zondervan.com/ebooks.

This title is also available in a Zondervan audio edition. Visit www.zondervan.fm.

Requests for information should be addressed to:

Zondervan, *Grand Rapids, Michigan 49530*

Library of Congress Cataloging-in-Publication Data

Willard, Timothy D.
    Veneer : living deeply in a surface society / Timothy D. Willard and R. Jason Locy.
      p. cm.
    Includes bibliographical references.
    ISBN 978-0-310-32563-5 (hardcover, jacketed)
    1. Christian life—United States. 2. Christianity and culture—United States. I.
Locy, R. Jason. II. Title.
BV4501.3.W544 2011
248.40973'090511—dc22   2010049394

Cover design: FiveStone.com
Interior design: Katherine Lloyd, The DESK

Printed in the United States of America

---

11 12 13 14 15 /DCI/ 23 22 21 20 19 18 17 16 15 14 13 12 11 10 9 8 7 6 5 4 3 2 1

To Christine and Heather
for keeping us grounded,
for speaking truth into our lives,
and for your unwavering support
and unveneered love

CONTENTS

Prelude

CRAZY BREED

The Language of Culture

THERE IS A DEEPER PORTION OF OUR BEING THAT WE RARELY
ALLOW OTHERS TO SEE. CALL IT A SOUL MAYBE; THIS IS THE PLACE
THAT HOLDS THE MOST VALUE. ALL ELSE CAN DRIFT BUT THIS.
WHEN THIS DIES OUR BODY HAS NO MEANING. WE HANDLE THIS
PORTION OF OUR BEING WITH EXTREME CARE. LIFE TEARS AT US AND
SCARS US AS CHILDREN, SO WE ADOPT FACADES AND MASKS TO HIDE THIS
PART OF US, TO KEEP THIS SACRED PART OF OURSELVES FROM THE PAIN.
AND YET, WE LONG TO COMMUNICATE THIS DEEPER PLACE ...
TO CONNECT WITH EACH OTHER ON THIS SPIRITUAL LEVEL,
FOR WE KNOW THAT THIS IS THE ONLY PART OF US THAT WILL LAST.

— Jon Foreman, Switchfoot

"It's perfect!" she shouts, peppering his neck with kisses.

And it does seem perfect, their little piece of heaven in the form of a small two-bedroom loft just outside of town. Her parents help them move in and surprise them with a table and couch. Pictures on the walls, old books on the shelves, and a small boxy TV on a rickety microwave stand they picked up at the thrift store – their modest belongings look sparse in the apartment. Just the way they like it.

As they unpack their wedding gifts, their playful laughter bounces off the pale walls, and they linger in the innocence of their vows. Theirs is a California kind of love – bright, sunny, and simple. They don't have much, yet they have all they need.

But time passes and so does the simplicity that marks their lives. Somewhere along the way, money shifts from a background thought to a necessity: one kid, two kids, a third, a bigger place, another car, a better job. He's gone more now, pursuing the next raise, the next position; she stays home. Their life together revolves around soccer games and school events, suburban basement wine parties

with friends, and over-the-top group vacations. The relentless demands of their schedule keep them exhausted, and
they barely have a chance to talk. The nights of lovemaking in the wee hours are transformed into estranged conversations as they lie in the dark a million miles from one
another. From the street, their house—their family—seems
perfect. And maybe they are. Maybe this is the inevitable
end to the whole thing.

He looks at his watch. It's 7:00 back home and the kids'
bedtime routine would be starting soon. Teeth brushed,
room picked up, story picked out, he would close the blinds
to keep the last rays of the summer sun from reaching into
the room. The kids would bounce around and finally land
in his lap, their warm bodies snuggled against him, their
flannel pajama bottoms soft against his hand as he'd pull
them close. They'd rub his scruffy cheek and he would
smile. "In the light of the moon a little egg lay on a leaf ..."[1]
"Read it again," they'd always whisper. And he would, followed by a kiss on the cheek, a "now I lay me down to
sleep," and an "I love you"—lights out.

But tonight, like a lot of nights, he's not home for the
goodnight ritual. Instead, he sits in a stuffy meeting room
clear across the country, closing the big deal. *This is life*, he
always reminds himself. A man has to work. He has to
make money. His wife "understands" and the kids don't

know any better. *Where does the time go? What am I chasing?* he wonders. And then he thinks of *her*—his love. Their relationship is strained; he knows their life isn't as fulfilling as it once was.

What have I done?

Back home, the kids finally asleep, she draws herself a bath. She looks in the mirror and notices that the young attractive woman in the wedding photographs, the newlywed who lived in that two-bedroom loft, is gone. Her youth and the man she once loved seem to have left one night without saying a word. The girls in the magazines, even the ones her age—*how do they do it?* All her friends had "the surgery" and their husbands loved it. Maybe it would revive her marriage. Maybe it would revive her heart?

After her bath she heads downstairs and, with no one to talk to, she flips the laptop open. Out there, in the land of tagged photos and "friends," she finds comfort, someone to connect with when he's not around. This may be *life*, but it's not the life she imagined. She always dreamed her life would somehow fly above all the stuff people clutter their lives with. She closes her eyes, gulps her merlot. *Is there a way out of the shallows?*

She cries just a little bit every day.

———

Each day – from morning toast to evening television – certain tensions surface. The life you want and the life you live cannot find each other. The world around you seems perfect, but your life feels like a wreck. A little part of you wants something more. You do all the right things: wear the right clothes, have the right job, live in the right neighborhood, but something's missing.

The promises of the world don't match up with what it actually delivers. We invest in our 401(k) only to watch it disappear. We get the job we want but still don't make enough money. We get rid of our wrinkles but still look old next to the pictures in the magazine.

If we listen closely, we can hear the world speaking a language, a language that echoes in the way we dress, the jobs we take, and even how we interact with our friends. It is the language of culture. We all speak this language as we mimic the world of *celebrity*, buy in to the promise of *consumption*, and place our trust in the hope of *progress*.

In the celebrity world, we are tempted by a lifestyle that puts the self above all others. We believe the tabloid lies that tell us visibility equals importance. And these feelings of importance resonate with us as we look for the approval of others.

Through consumption, we search for meaning. We let ad agencies and marketers define us. We think that if we buy certain things, then the world will accept us. On the outside, we look perfect, but on the inside, the search continues.

The progress of the technological world allows us to escape the real. Our computer screens and avatars simulate the life we want but not necessarily the life we have. The true us becomes hidden in exchange for our brighter online projection.

But what does it mean to believe the promises of the world? Can we find our way back to the simplicity of the two-bedroom loft?

Many of us will find ourselves in a scenario similar to the California lovers, if we are not there already. The ideals and dreams—the "something deeper"—we held on to from a more innocent time will fade, drowned out by the language of culture.

And yet hope persists, drawing us away from this scenario. It exists in another language that empowers us to resist the language of culture. Through this language we discover how relationships form our very lives, inside and out; we uncover a love that calls us beyond ourselves; we begin to understand what it means to abide with one another and with God. We see, finally, that when we view our lives through the lens of holy redemption, we have no use for veneer.

Chapter One

SAWMILL

Seeing the Veneer

THOU ART THE GO-BETWEEN OF RUSTIC LOVERS;

THY WHITE BARK HAS THEIR SECRETS IN ITS KEEPING;

REUBEN WRITES HERE THE HAPPY NAME OF PATIENCE,

AND THY LITHE BOUGHS HANG MURMURING AND WEEPING

ABOVE HER, AS SHE STEALS THE MYSTERY FROM THY KEEPING.

— *James Russell Lowell, "The Birch Tree"*

If you ever visit Pennsylvania Amish country, you might happen upon a little town called Lititz, a place where old men like to sit and talk about the weather, and old women like to sit and talk about old men.[1] At first glance, the town appears to be a simple place with not much to see or do. But once you find your way around, you realize the town is a hidden gem. A quaint main street with some local merchants and more coffee shops than coffee drinkers presents the quintessential spirit of Americana. Like most small towns, the tourist draws are a bit unusual: the oldest pretzel factory, the oldest girls' boarding school, and the second oldest chocolate factory in the country.

Lititz Springs Park acts as the epicenter of town, giving the locals a natural spring and the ducks a place to get free bread. A replica old-world train station was built at the front of the park to mark the history of the railway that cuts the town in half. The park amphitheater always has something going on. The most popular event each year is the Fourth of July celebration when visitors from all over the country fill the park grounds during the holiday week to catch a glimpse of concerts, car shows, comedians. The celebration week culminates with the Queen of Candles ceremony. Thousands of floating candles are lit in the canal that runs the length of the park as one of the high school senior hopefuls receives the crown. An epic fireworks display follows, the final touch to one of the oldest Fourth of July celebrations in the country.

On the other side of the railway sits the Wilbur Chocolate factory. The weathered redbrick building stands five stories tall with a small gift shop on the first floor where locals and tourists can read up on chocolate, see how it's made, and, for fifteen dollars, buy enough of it to bake Christmas cookies this year and next. The aroma of chocolate that fills the air is the only fragrance that stands a chance against the smell of the Amish farms that surround the area.

If you want to catch the true vibe of the town, show up at Tomato Pie café any morning around 9:00. You can seat yourself at a table or sit at the original 1950s-style bar where the grizzled locals sip their coffee. All the things you aren't supposed to talk about, they do. Opinions on religion and politics are passed around as much as the sugar for the coffee. In the evening, a younger crowd fills the space, hopping on free wi-fi and suffering through homework. The café manages to seamlessly fuse the old with the new.

On the outskirts of the town, past the shops of Main Street, you'll find what appears to be a wood junkyard — piles of old lumber stacked everywhere in no obvious pattern. From the entrance, the wood looks like stuff to be thrown away, wood that has lost its purpose. But a survey of the property reveals hundred-year-old barn timber going through the brutal process of finding new life. This junkyard turns out to be a working sawmill.

Dean Brandt runs this wood salvage operation. He collects antique wood, selling it as some of the most beautiful hardwood flooring you can buy. His father, Sylvan, who began the business decades earlier, coined the business's motto: "We don't offer perfection but, rather, the beauty of imperfection."

Dean scours the country looking for wood that comes from dilapidated barns and old farmhouses, weathered wood that most people send to the scrap pile. The wood's patina tells the story of the mature tree that produced it, as well as the story of how the wood was used. You can't buy timber like this at the lumber store; trees are harvested when they're young, so they aren't old enough to produce a rich character.

You can tell a lot about a tree by looking at its rings. The waves and lines reflect the tree's life — a fire, a disease, or a storm that bent the tree over or caused it to lose a branch. If a few of the rings are close together, then it was a dry season and the tree didn't grow much. The farther apart the rings, the more it rained, the more the tree grew. As the tree aged, its character deepened, as evidenced by the unique lifeline of its rings.

When Dean and his crew find this patinaed wood, the time-intensive process of giving it new life begins. They hand-strip each beam of the nails, staples, and other pieces of metal embedded in the grain. Sometimes this takes more than two hours. Then they rough-saw the beams with the massive sawmill blade and place the fresh-cut boards in a kiln for drying. The two-week drying process sucks out moisture and shrinks the boards.

After the crew retrieves the rough-cut boards from the kiln, they run them through a twin-blade saw known as a gang rip, which cuts the boards into various widths. Finally, the boards are run through a molder that simultaneously cuts the tongue and groove needed to piece the flooring together, while also planing both top and bottom of the board. The operation takes patience and hard work. But in the end, the reclaiming process reveals the antique wood's beauty, its rich grain enhanced by the hand of time.

Distressed wood and vintage furniture are popular. On any given day, you can flip on the television and see an interior designer showing you how to distress a piece of wood. He takes a new piece of wood or furniture and tries to make it look old by hitting it with a hammer or a chain. To Dean, this is wood heresy because there is no story to tell.

Telling someone you beat your coffee table with a chain is a little different from telling them the coffee table was made from one of the doors to your granddad's farmhouse, the same door that he carried your grandma through after he returned home from the Second World War and the same door that was on the house that your mom grew up in. The story of the wood makes it unique, and so you appreciate the scratches and the dents and the imperfections of the coffee table. Dean calls these blemishes the memory of the wood, beauty marks that contribute to the wood's uniqueness. "The beauty of imperfection."

———

In the back of most Home Depots, past the lawn mowers and lightbulbs and refrigerators, you'll find the wood flooring section. The display shows a few samples and gives the price per square foot along with a flowery description. Employees, however, don't plane the wood in the back room or cure it for any length of time, and it was not salvaged from a hundred-year-old farmhouse.

This type of wood looks real and feels real. But does real wood come in the same colors as a J.Crew sweater? The flooring that fills this aisle is engineered. It has a veneer, a thin covering that hides the real material underneath. Manufacturers do this to make the wood look expensive without the consumer having to pay for the real thing. They inflate the perceived value of the product by hiding inferior wood under a veneer.

But the flooring at Home Depot isn't the only thing that uses a veneer to give itself value. Like engineered flooring, people apply a veneer. Embarrassed by the scars of our humanity, we try to hide our brokenness. We use a veneer to cover over ourselves, hoping others will perceive us as having greater worth, as being more beautiful and perfect than we feel inside. Most of the time, we aren't aware that we're doing it; our culture is so glossed over with the sheen of fake perfection that we unknowingly comply.

Some of us will go to any lengths to hide ourselves and create a false identity. It's what we know because it's who we've become. Fashion designer Tom Ford looks at the American woman today and doesn't recognize what he sees. He says, "I don't understand all these breasts right now, and they don't look like breasts. They look like someone's taken a grapefruit half and inserted it under your skin … We're starting to think that this is what women should look like … You're beautiful, you're glossy, you're shiny, but you're not human."[2]

We whiten our teeth, color our hair, tuck our tummies, and cut open our breasts to insert silicone. We inject chemicals into our cheeks and lips and eyebrows. We buy fancy shoes made from Italian leather, buy cars that cost more than our parents' houses, and go to jobs that suck the life out of us but pay great. We update Facebook with photos of all the interesting places we visit, and accumulate followers on Twitter who, apparently, are waiting to know what we ate for breakfast.

But have we ever stopped to reflect on any of this? Why do we want to look like the person in the magazine? Why do we want a better job or more money? What about social networking draws us to spend more time adjusting our profiles than talking to human people? Do we associate our identity, our worth, with physical attributes and objects like perfect white teeth, wealth, or the accumulation of nice things? Sadly, many of us do. We errantly think that by enhancing the physical, we will be able to find or communicate who we are to this great big world. After all, in advanced Western society, it seems expected that we inflate – or veneer – our selves in order to achieve recognition. Most people understand and accept this practice. It's part of the language of culture.

But the more we veneer, the more comfortable our lives seem. When a whole society craves superficial beauty, instant gratification, and comfortable living, it's difficult not to play along in the charade. We are a people who, at the click of a mouse, can have everything we could possibly want but nothing we need. Philosopher Peter Kreeft observes, "There is something radically wrong with a civilization in which millions devote their lives to pointless luxuries that do not even make them happy."[3] We look to these luxuries to make life livable and to make ourselves feel as if we belong. But if we survey our society—the wealthiest in the world—we will find it rife with people who are struggling with depression and despair, hopelessness and lack of purpose, void of true identity.

As Christians, the idea of veneer goes against our core beliefs. One of our foundational beliefs is that we are broken, that we don't have it all together and that we need Christ; he gives us our identity. If this is true, and if the acceptance of this compelled us to follow Christ, then why do we try so hard to live as if we aren't broken?

Brennan Manning talks about this in his book *The Importance of Being Foolish*. He says the crisis of American spirituality is that the battle between wanting things of the flesh and surrendering to the Spirit is too much for Christians. Too often the flesh wins, and because of this, we lose sight of the fact that we are children of God. "It is not that I am afraid to tell you who I am; I truly cannot tell you because I don't know myself who I am. God calls me by name, and I do not answer because I do not know my name."[4]

As followers of the Way, we have veered off course. We have become content to ape a culture that loves the self, merely going with the flow instead of cutting a new path through this inflated faux society. Instead of finding our identity in Christ, we have looked to veneer.

Pastor Eugene Peterson describes his fellow Christian brothers and sisters as "uncritically embracing the ways and means practiced by the high-profile men and women who lead large corporations, congregations, nations, and causes, people who show us how to make money, win wars, manage people, sell products, manipulate emotions, and who then write books and give lectures telling us how we can do what they are doing."[5]

Peterson's comments give us a clue as to how our world works and, more important, how it talks. As Christians, we end up believing in the distorted notion that physical beauty and the accumulation of fine things that the rest of the world seeks equals worth, equals identity. But for Christians, beauty has little to do with physical expressions and everything to do with the spiritual.

True beauty, some say, resides at the threshold of pain. This is why we can call the crucifixion beautiful. Not because we are barbarians, but because there's an inherent truth and goodness in it. Christ lays his life down for all of humankind, past, present, and future. This is good; *he* is good. And his goodness points us to truth, truth of redemption, truth of coming restoration, truth of forgiveness.

This is why we can look back on pain in our lives and call it beautiful. It wasn't beautiful then; it was hell. But from that hell grew a shoot, and from that shoot a leaf, and life sprang up where hell resided; that's beautiful. God makes it so.

We usually don't understand this kind of beauty in a person, but when we come across someone who is content with his true self, we are drawn to him. He is that rare person who emanates beauty through his approach to life, a beauty that comes from within, like the beauty of antique wood. We admire this. We wonder how nothing in society really touches him; he seems to walk between raindrops. We can't put our finger on what makes him so special. It's something altogether vibrant, something that inspires us to be better sons and daughters, husbands and wives – better people.

If you drive to old Pumping Station Road just north of Lititz, you'll find a trailhead that leads out into the Pennsylvania State Game Lands. Locals use this trail to go hunting, ride mountain bikes, and enjoy the scenery. Back in the day, before Dean took over the sawmill, he and his friends partied in those woods. But over time, the partying got old. He started looking for God, or maybe God started looking for him. About the time Dean was in his thirties, they finally met. Like many of us, Dean met God with half a lifetime of baggage. The hurt from fractured relationships, the tensions within his family, the emptiness that comes along with years of hard partying — all the junk that scarred his life, like the memory lines of wood — was now in the redeeming hands of God.

If you were to meet Dean now, the first thing he would do is offer you a cigar. The second thing he would do is light it for you. Dean doesn't dabble in small talk. He has a way of always getting to something a little deeper. He likes to focus his conversation on the things that matter most in his life: God, family, and antique wood.

Of course, the fragments of his misspent youth linger. Like an old knee injury that moans every time it rains, Dean's past still creaks every now and then, but Dean's sense of commitment to God and his pursuit of an honest life prevail.

Dean lives with a righteous grit. When you look into his eyes, he doesn't look away. When you ask him a question, he'll shoot you straight. He doesn't bother trying to dazzle you with what he thinks impresses you. What you see is what you get.

As he continues to grow in his relationship with God, Dean finds more meaning in his work. He's figured out that time shapes a person, but that God has the power to reclaim a person. So it's fitting that Dean works with old barn wood. He understands it. He reaches back into the past — a time traveler of sorts — and revives a forgotten beauty. Dean loves living in this strange land of rejected barn wood; maybe he loves it because he understands the worth of the dejected and damaged. It seems that people like Dean are always the quickest to seize meaning when they find it. They're the ones who see value in discarded things when the crowd obsesses over the bright and shiny.

It's one thing to fail and to experience loss or embarrassment. We all do that. It's quite another to wear it on your sleeve. And that's what Dean does, not because he's proud of it but because he knows that the redeemed grime of his past makes him beautiful today.

Chapter Two

CELEBRITY ME

Wanting Our Fifteen Minutes of Fame

ABOVE ALL, LET THERE BE ENOUGH LIVE ACTION!
THEY LIKE TO WATCH, AND THAT'S THE CHIEF ATTRACTION.
WITH LOTS OF THINGS BEFORE THEIR EYES DISPLAYED
FOR CROWDS TO STARE AND GAPE IN WONDER OF,
THERE'S MOST OF YOUR SUCCESS ALREADY
AND YOU'RE THE MAN WHOM THEY WILL LOVE.
BY MASS ALONE THE MASSES CAN BE WON.

– Goethe, Faust

"That's hot!" It was the catchphrase of the 2000s. Coined by blonde socialite Paris Hilton on her reality TV show *The Simple Life*, the phrase became the oft-repeated staple of office one-liners. The jet-setting heiress to the Hilton hotel fortune had never worked a "real job" in her life, but her over-the-top spending and partying made her a household name and landed her the reality show.

The media can't resist telling the wild stories of how Paris handles her inheritance. Gossip columns and magazines regularly feature pictures of Paris parading from red-carpet events to fashion shows to A-list parties. Magazines like *Vanity Fair*, *GQ*, *Rolling Stone*, *Vogue*, and *People* feature her on their covers. She has written books, starred in movies and television shows, and recorded an album. A pop-culture icon, Paris is the quintessential modern celebrity: a person who has a life the public watches.[1]

Stand in the checkout lane of the grocery store, turn on the television, or surf the internet, and you will find no shortage of celebrity "news." If it's not Paris on the cover, then the headlines are about Angelina or Cruise or whomever.

US Weekly, National Enquirer, Entertainment Tonight, and *TMZ* all serve up the latest dish on what's hot, or not, in Hollywood. As a nation, our new favorite pastime is keeping up with the people we view on the screen, the lives of actors and actresses and athletes and musicians reported to us as if their lives are a movie to be watched.

Brad Pitt takes his shirt off in a hotel room in *Thelma and Louise*. He goes fly-fishing with his brother in *A River Runs Through It*. He goes crazy in *12 Monkeys*. He is a con artist in *Ocean's Eleven*. An outlaw, an old man, a Nazi killer – in role after role, his good looks and acting chops turn movies into blockbusters.

But our obsession goes beyond his film appearances. The media report on his relationship with Gwyneth. They split. He marries Jennifer. They divorce. He moves in with Angelina. The paparazzi capture it all through their grainy lenses—the relationships, the adoptions, the post-Katrina homes – as we follow Pitt's life story. At some point we start paying less attention to Pitt's talent and more attention to his "real" life.

The media portrays the celebrity life as the epitome of success. Entertainment news flaunt images of expensive cars, designer dresses, and exotic travels of the celebrity. Magazines feature pictures of their homes alongside decorating tips. Their bodies are scrutinized and promoted as "perfect." It seems as if the celebrity has the "easy life" we all daydream about.

When *People* first launched in 1974, the magazine reached a circulation of 1.25 million within ten months and recorded a profit within eighteen months. The selection process by which *People*'s editor chose a successful cover contains vivid insight into what the media sells: "Young is better than old. Pretty is better than ugly. Rich is better than poor. TV is better than music. Music is better than movies. Movies are better than sports. Anything is better than politics. And nothing is better than a celebrity who has just died."[2]

Sitting at home, leading a comparatively normal life, we fantasize about the young, pretty, rich people we see in the magazines. As we thumb through the pages of magazines like *People*, we plug ourselves into their narrative. We think about what we would wear or whom we would date or where we would vacation. These thoughts, coupled with the image of success implied by the media, lead us to long for the celebrity life. In his book *Empire of Illusion*, Pulitzer Prize–winning author Chris Hedges writes, "Celebrities, who often come from humble backgrounds, are held up as proof that anyone, even we, can be adored by the world … Our fantasies of belonging, of fame, of success, and of fulfillment, are projected onto celebrities."[3]

———

Sports icon Tiger Woods led the life most men dream about. He was the private family guy who showed up on the weekends and played golf better than anyone else on the course.

But that all changed when Woods rammed his Cadillac Escalade into a tree. According to some reports, he was driving away from his wife, who found out he had cheated on her. A swarm of reporters camped out at the Woods' Florida estate to cover the story. And over the next couple of weeks, the media discovered and reported his extramarital affairs. Months later, his iconic image was tarnished forever; he checked himself into a sexual addiction rehabilitation clinic, and his marriage crumbled.

The news of Woods' affairs was jarring. The real Woods had just trumped the version we bought into. Shocked and bothered, we learned that we foolishly believed the veneer of Woods' life. When we hear a story like Woods', our perception of reality is shattered; we tune in even more to find out the real story. Realizing that Woods' image was false doesn't diminish the story for us; it makes it grander.

Megan Fox, the sexy star we saw bending over the hood of a Camero in the first *Transformers* movie, knows the act of a real person versus a character well. In her public life, she projects an image that will sell movie tickets or increase ratings or move magazines off of shelves. In an interview with the *New York Times*, Fox explains how, in the media, she uses various characters in different situations, noting that "it's a testament to my real personality that I would go so far as to make up another personality to give to the world. The reality is, I'm hidden amongst all the insanity. Nobody can find me."[4]

Fox realizes that if she wants to find success, she needs to differentiate herself from the rest of the personalities in Hollywood. She perceives this as savvy business sense, and most would agree. The article goes on to explain that Fox's tabloid narrative differs from the stories of other actresses; it's not so much about who she is dating as much as it's about her extreme personality. "You have to be put in a box in this industry so they can sell you," Fox continues. "They need to get hits on their blogs or sell their magazines. So everyone is something. And if I'm not a party girl, which I'm not, I then have to be the outrageous personality."

As it turns out, the life that the media *and* the celebrity portray isn't always real. Publicists, managers, and lawyers carefully script the celebrity life to control public perception. In the same way that an actor plays a character on-screen, celebrities act their own roles in life—the boy next door or the wild party girl—their personas projected through magazines, television, and blogs by publishers, publicists, and press agents.

———

"Meet Julia Allison," the headline reads. "She can't act. She can't sing. She's not rich. But thanks to a genius for self-promotion—plus Flickr, Twitter, and her blogs—she's become an Internet celebrity. How she did it—and how you can too." This was the teaser for *Wired* magazine's feature article about a woman named Julia Allison. She graced the cover in her sexed-up style, with an equally provocative article layout conveying the idea that she is a celebrity. But is she really?

Julia represents a fabricated expression of her true self. She leverages the internet through constant blogging and twittering to achieve celebrity status. Her trick "is to think of herself as the subject of a magazine profile, with every post or update adding dimensions to her as a character. 'I treat it like a fire,' she says. 'You have to add logs, or it'll be like one of those YouTube videos that flame out.'"[5]

And, for Julia, the self-promotion pays off. She has twenty-two thousand Twitter followers. Her Facebook page boasts approximately sixty thousand fans. Her Lifecast—a constant stream of press clippings, photos, videos, musings, and miscellany Julia finds interesting—shows pictures of her with movie stars and at gala events. A self-described "professional talking head," in one year she appeared on television three hundred and fifty times.

Because of the success of people like Julia Allison, celebrity status is fair game to anyone with a laptop and web camera. We can all fabricate publicity stunts and manipulate pictures to become someone we are not. Everyone feels entitled to their 15MB of fame.

We find ourselves living within a society with the unprecedented ability to broadcast our lives through reality shows and YouTube videos, which have helped create a world that rewards the constant exposure of self. Modern man wants to feel recognized and visible and connected. He does this either on a mass scale, by trying to be on television, or on a smaller scale, through social networking sites.[6] The more followers we have, the more important we must be. The acceptance validates us. In our effort to be known, we can use the computer to manufacture a personality, becoming whomever we want.

Life on the computer screen permits us to "project ourselves into our own dramas, dramas in which we are producer, director, and star … Computer screens are the new location for our fantasies, both erotic and intellectual."[7] So we live in two worlds. We all wake up and brush our teeth and head to work. We get into real cars and have real families and friends. We go to high school football games, attend college, and get promotions. This world is very real.

The other world, however, lives primarily in the ether and in our minds. We see images on the television and the movie screen, we visit websites and blogs and follow people on Twitter, and suddenly this virtual world emerges. It's all towers of fame and wealth, and everything we could ever want stands in full view, staring us down, beckoning us. And so we indulge, plunging into the celebrity culture so we can escape the real world. We wake up, spread the preserves on our toast, and head out for another day, all the while envisioning what it would be like to live like someone who doesn't exist: Celebrity Me.

―――――

After Jesus is baptized, he walks off to be alone in the wilderness.[8] He fasts and prays for forty days. Alone and hungry, Jesus finds himself tempted with the same things that tempt us in the celebrity world. "The dread and intelligent spirit"[9] entices Jesus with wealth and celebrity and glory.

"You are the Son of God," says the dread spirit. "Turn that stone into bread." With the point of a finger or the flicker of a thought, Jesus could easily turn stone to bread.

After all, later in his life, he turns water to wine and feeds five thousand with a boy's lunch. But Jesus doesn't need the bread. "Man does not live on bread alone,"[10] he answers. The world thinks we need abundance. It thinks we need wealth. Success. But no matter what the bread of society looks like, Jesus says, "No thanks." Our sustenance is found in God.

The tempter comes back with another test. "Throw yourself off this cliff. Call on the angels; they can save you." If Jesus were to dive off the cliff and if angels were to save him, the story of his grand escape would spread quickly. Jesus would become an instant celebrity. He would be loved and revered and worshiped. Certainly, he could skip the whole messy business of the crucifixion. But Jesus shuns the spotlight; he doesn't need the fame.

The tempter, a persistent bugger, returns a third time to show Jesus all the kingdoms of the land and their splendor. "All of this," he says, "I will give you. Just worship me." Jesus simply has to deny his Father and the tempter will give him wealth, fame, and power. But Jesus doesn't need a shortcut to glory. And so Jesus looks at his tempter and says, "Get away from me. You must serve God alone."

And that's that; the tempter leaves Jesus.

Jesus' response to the temptations he faced presents a stark contrast to the celebrity culture. As Jesus' life unfolds, we see a man who sought the fame of his Father. Jesus shows us that those who follow him are called to seek not visibility but anonymity; "if anyone wants to be first, he must be the very last, and the servant of all."[11] A caveat to this verse does not exist; the path Jesus sets before his disciples winds into the narrows.

As Christians, many of us attempt to justify the pursuit of success as the world defines it. "It can't be wrong to establish a bit of celebrity to obtain true influence," we say. It's a noble pursuit, right? But if we look around, we will always find someone with more money or more power or more fame. Success defined by the world's standards leads down a path lined with anxiety and self-doubt.

Inherent in Jesus' confrontation with Satan in the wilderness we see Jesus' antidote for the lure of celebrity. In each response to the tempter Jesus shows us that true success, the kind God cares about, is the freedom of not feeling trapped by the rules of worldly success. And that freedom comes from obedience to the Father.

In his wilderness temptation, in his teaching, and in his prayer in Gethsemane, Jesus defers to God's will. "I came down from heaven not to follow my own whim," says Jesus, "but to accomplish the will of the One who sent me."[12] What if we began to defer the so-called opportunities to increase our own celebrity to God the Father? What might we find? Would we find a freedom to be the person God intended us to be? "We are not responsible for success," writes theologian Klaus Bockmuehl, "but we remain responsible for obedience."[13] What God creates with our obedience is his concern, not ours.

But we tend to choke on this kind of wisdom. The Christian leader often struggles to understand this, desiring the notoriety associated with worldly success. They think that because a person *can* create a celebrity persona, they should, and that once they obtain fame and wealth and power, they will leverage it all for the good of Christendom. The Christian leader, it seems, has fallen prey to the dread spirit, believing that in order to win the world, we must speak its language, forgetting that Christian leadership is not about "power and control, but a leadership of powerlessness and humility."[14] But not all of us struggle with the temptations that come with leading people. For many of us, our temptations emerge in the subtleties of popularity or the cool factor in how we dress. One way or another, the "look at me, I'm someone" complex surfaces. But somewhere in our heart of hearts, we hear the still, small voice that whispers, "It's a sham."

In some way, we all face the temptations of the dread spirit just as Jesus did. But we must remain obedient, just as Jesus was, recognizing the temptations as cheap versions of the truth. As James the apostle reminds us, true religion "guard(s) against corruption from the godless world."[15] We either obey, and conform to the will of the Father, or we conform to the world.

In C. S. Lewis's classic *The Screwtape Letters*, we see uncommon insight into the lies of the tempter. The book is a fictional exchange of letters between a newly recruited demon, Wormwood, and his uncle Screwtape, an old pro. The elder Screwtape gives expert advice to his nephew, instructing him on how to trip up a new Christian convert. The advice centers on sidetracking the convert from the joy and blessed life found in God and, as a result, rendering his faith impotent.

In one letter, Screwtape warns Wormwood of the obedience that God demands of his followers. "But the obedience which the Enemy [God] demands of men is quite a different thing," says Uncle Screwtape. "One must face the fact that all the talk of perfect freedom, is not (as one would gladly believe) mere propaganda, but an appalling truth. He really does want to fill the universe with a lot of loathsome little replicas of Himself—creatures whose life, on its miniature scale, will be qualitatively like His own, not because He has absorbed them but because their wills freely conform to His."[16]

———

In the veneer of celebrity, we find ourselves striving after the world's idea of success, which elevates the self. When we buy into the veneer, we begin living life with a focus that zooms squarely on the individual. What the individual wears, what they drive, how they behave define their success. In the elevation of such things, we see an unhealthy emphasis on the self take shape. We feel unsatisfied unless we have influence over others. We feel irritated unless others approve of us. We feel discontented unless we receive recognition in our work. Influence, approval, achievement; in the celebrity world, these are our idols.[17]

Theologian John Calvin is often quoted as saying that our hearts are perpetual idol factories.[18] This seems especially true in our celebrity culture, where the pursuit of self moves us farther from God and closer to loneliness; he fades as the star of self shines bright. Jewish philosopher Martin Buber comments, "Something has stepped between our existence and God to shut off the light of heaven … [and] that something is in fact ourselves, our own bloated selfhood."[19]

But no matter how hard we try, an idol cannot fulfill our need for God — a real, living, intimate God. We need our God to be accessible, not with the on-off button of a remote control but through relationship. "An idol leads a man, by necessity, into loneliness," writes Bockmuehl, "when what man needs is a god with whom he can have dialogue."[20]

The God of Abraham does not lead anyone into loneliness. He leads us into himself. He calls each by name toward himself, the essence of all that is good and holy, full of fear and wonder. This is where he calls you. It's a place where the self decreases and God increases.

As Christians, we are to seek the good of others above our own. Dietrich Bonhoeffer in *The Cost of Discipleship* presents the question, "How then do the disciples [of Jesus] differ from the heathen? What does it really mean to be a Christian?"[21] He answers this with the word *perissos*, or "extraordinary." But his use of the word *extraordinary* is not how we normally define it. Bonhoeffer uses it as a term for uncommon living. Christians are called to go beyond what is expected in society.[22]

If the world expects that we promote ourselves in order to achieve fame or make more money, then to be extraordinary, according to Bonhoeffer, is to seek that which is uncommon. Instead of doing whatever it takes to make more money, we give more away. Instead of elevating ourselves so others perceive us as great, we elevate others in their endeavors; we serve them.

Being extraordinary in our faith is being the light that

shines before the world. Bonhoeffer reminds us that it's not that we *have* light; it's that we *are* the light. We are, therefore, visible to the world, loving our neighbor, caring for the widow and the orphan, forsaking all to know him. These and other actions should make us visible. They are selfless actions, actions that tell the world our care is not about fame; it is about the extraordinary. All else is advertising.

Bonhoeffer continues, "The better righteousness [that which is extraordinary] of the disciples must have a motive which lies beyond self. Of course it has to be visible, but they must take care that it does not become visible simply for the sake of becoming visible."[23]

So it comes to motive. In our brokenness, the celebrity motive compels us to be known. In our humility, the Christian motive compels us to be hidden – in Christ. When we attempt to communicate like the world, be cool like the world, use the same devices to become popular, are we being extraordinary? Or are we merely rising to the world's standard, which goes no farther than self-glorification?

There is no room in the Christian life for pursuit of celebrity. It doesn't make sense. Instead, Christ should shape our narrative. The story he writes does not look like one of celebrity fame and fortune but instead one of humility, giving, sacrifice, selflessness, and honesty. In this realization, we begin to find our way. We begin to see that compared with the spectacle of celebrity, our life is extraordinary.

Chapter Three

THE QUEEN IS DEAD – LONG LIVE THE QUEEN

Recognizing Consumption

SOCIETY IS COMMONLY CHEAP.
WE MEET AT VERY SHORT INTERVALS NOT HAVING HAD
TIME TO ACQUIRE ANY NEW VALUE FOR EACH OTHER.

– Henry David Thoreau, Walden

On the heels of the Protestant Reformation, Queen Elizabeth's empire heaved with massive religious tensions and war; she found that the country needed a unifying force, an icon that would bring majesty back to the throne and confidence to the people. She would become that icon. She would take no husband and instead would marry herself to England. She became the Virgin Queen, a godlike figure the people loved and cherished.

She was the embodiment of an empire and took special care to present herself to the public accordingly. "She was presented," writes biographer Christopher Hibbert, "as an ageless, gorgeously clad figure being carried along in majesty, sitting enthroned upon a triumphal cart beneath an embroidered canopy." In her processions, she was flanked by knights, with each detail of her presentation scripted to invoke the wonder and awe of a goddess. Elizabeth's public persona was "a brilliant exercise in propaganda."[1]

Along with her manipulative public presentations, Elizabeth was renowned for her extravagant spending. Sociologists tell of her lavish "anti-supper" where guests

were escorted into an ornate dining hall with expensive
table dressings along with a spread of expensive foods.
Once guests were seated, servants removed everything in
an impressive fashion only to replace it with the real, and
equally lavish, dinner.[2]

The queen used her spending to control her kingdom.
Her lavishness, especially in the context of royal ceremony,
proved the legitimacy of her monarchy. It empowered her
to create "a vast theater devoted to the aggrandizement
[increasing] of her power as a monarch."[3]

At the same time, the noblemen were wasting their
wealth in order to please the queen. To meet expectations
of what it meant to serve in the court, and to keep up with
the "social competition" within the court, the nobles were
forced to "spend with a new enthusiasm."[4] The mindset
of veneer took hold, and the true selves of the noblemen
became secondary to their perceived value in the court.

Prior to the reign of Queen Elizabeth, the noble families
reserved the consumption of goods for items that benefited
the family's name and legacy. New goods were not considered valuable per se, only old ones that stood the test
of time. The shift to enthusiastic spending by the nobles
sparked a change in history – and in mentality. Items began
to be purchased for the immediate gratification of personal
status instead of family heritage.

Through this, Queen Elizabeth made a major discovery: our purchases communicate something. She realized she could manipulate people's perceptions with spending. This period in time marks what some sociologists believe to be the birth of modern consumption.[5] Elizabeth's style of governing had lasting effects on the broader culture as consumption eventually became a dynamic part of society.

But this was just the beginning. The consumer practices that began with Elizabeth stayed in elite circles at first, and it was not until the eighteenth century that the trickle-down effect of consumption fully blossomed. The Industrial Revolution was underway, with the consumer revolution occurring alongside it. During this time in England, culture began to be driven by marketplace sensibilities. By now people felt a heightened pressure to buy for self. With industry creating jobs, the elite fashion designers determining clothing trends, and a rising middle class, the time was ripe for a true consumer culture.[6]

Soon, marketplace manipulation was in full swing. Those who produced goods watched how the effect of purchasing impacted certain goods over others. They began to exploit this phenomenon for their own gain, targeting certain groups with specific goods. As sociologist Grant McCracken explains, "This new attention to and manipulation of the regularities of society helped propel the West forward and create new and more intimate connections between consumption and culture."[7] Producers, who created goods that — in some way — gave meaning or value to particular people, exploited the purchasing tendencies of the masses. This was the birth of modern-day marketing.

———

"The late twentieth century," writes sociologist David Lyon, "is witness to unprecedented evaporation of the grounds of meaning. The quest for some division between the real and the unreal, or even the true and untrue, moral and immoral, is futile."[8]

Through advertising, we see how blurry the lines of truth and fiction become. The Emmy Award – winning show *Mad Men* chronicles the lives and work of 1960s ad men at Sterling Cooper, a fictitious New York City ad agency. In one episode, the men of Sterling Cooper highlight their slanted view of truth when they develop a new ad campaign for Lucky Strike cigarettes. The campaign includes a new slogan, "It's Toasted." But when the executives at Lucky Strike are presented with the new slogan, they do not understand. The executives point out that all cigarettes are toasted, so why would they use that as a slogan? It is nothing unique to their process.

But that is not the point of advertising. The point of advertising is to take something true and exaggerate it or claim it as truth before someone else does. It does not matter if all cigarettes are toasted; if Lucky Strike says it first, then it becomes true only of them by implying that their cigarettes have something that other cigarettes do not.

This fictional *Mad Men* episode is based on the real-life Lucky Strike slogan. Daniel Boorstin, in his 1961 book, *The Image*, uses Lucky Strikes to make the point that by claiming a general truth to be particular to your product, the statement then becomes a quasi truth. He says that for advertisements, "The credibility cannot exist without the 'truth'; the seduction cannot exist without the 'falsehood.'"[9] Good ads live in a space where a little bit of truth is sprinkled with a little bit of lie so that the whole ad is believable.

In the consumer world run by marketers, we find it hard to locate the truth. And with techniques like product placement — companies paying to have their products placed on the set or in the story line of a TV show, movie, or book — we find it increasingly difficult to know when we are being sold something. No one can escape the five thousand ads that inundate our lives each day.[10]

Like Queen Elizabeth, marketers prefer the language of manipulation. They place perception over reality through a constant barrage of advertisements from the 33.7 billion dollar per year industry.[11] A consumer culture revolves around manipulation – of your emotions, of the truth, of reality, all to sell more products in a culture obsessed with consuming. We manipulate our way toward a bigger and brighter future, noblemen in the court of society, just trying to keep up.

When Levi Strauss first introduced jeans to America, his sales pitch was simple: durable pants for working-class folks. Strauss didn't give too much thought to fashion – jeans were a work garment for gold miners in the West. No one really cared much about what they looked like; they just needed to function.

But over time, things changed. A certain subculture of teens adopted jeans as a symbol of rebellion. They appeared in movies and magazines, worn by Kerouac, Dean, and Brando. They were worn less for their ability to handle a hard day's work and more as the anti-something.

Then, in 1980, a fifteen-year-old Brooke Shields slid on a pair of boots, unbuttoned her shirt, and posed in a pair of Calvin Klein's. With the flash of a camera, designer jeans became a must-have for women.

When Calvin Klein ran his first of many controversial print ads, he didn't pay attention to how his jeans held up in the fields; he just cared about how they looked. He understood that people were looking for ways to express themselves, and that if an identity statement could be made with his jeans, more people would buy them. Today, we seldom buy jeans for their durability; we buy them to tell the world something about us. We are a beatnik poet, a rebel without a cause, a greaser, the girl wanting to impress the boy; our choice of jeans, the cut and color and brand, speaks the language of culture without saying a word.

Whether we intend to or not, when we consume, we communicate several things about ourselves: our wealth, our personality, our affinities, and even our intelligence. Whether it is Levis or Diesel, McCafe or Starbucks, Mercedes or Chevy, Nike or Converse, every consumptive decision makes a statement. Consumption and identity have dangerously coalesced.[12]

In 2009, *Advertising Age* named Apple CEO Steve Jobs the marketing executive of the decade. This distinction means that Jobs can effectively communicate that a Mac is more than hard drives and memory and motherboards slipped inside a metal case. He is the epitome of the modern-day marketer.

Mac commercials paint their users as cool; they get it. The trendy music with stylized graphics and dancing silhouettes promote a sense of exuberance and playfulness. The young guy with jeans, T-shirt, and sneakers appears laid back and confident compared with the PC, a nerd in a wrinkled brown suit. Since they first aired, the Mac ads have made a statement. Over time, they have left little room for argument; no matter our computing preference, we believe the Mac to be cooler than the PC. Accurate or not, this perception becomes reality.

When we go to the store, we consider what we would rather be associated with: cool guy or nerd guy. We all like to be associated with the in-crowd, so we want to buy the Mac. With our new Macs on our laps, we think people will see us as one of the cool kids. Marketing insiders applaud Jobs' ability to *brand* his products.

Scott Bedbury, the guru behind brands like Nike and Starbucks, says, "branding is about taking something common and improving upon it in ways that make it more valuable and meaningful."[13] A shoe is just a shoe. But when Nike can motivate us toward physical fitness and a healthy lifestyle and ultimately to buy their product, the brand takes shape. The feeling of health and fitness we feel after buying the shoe, even though we may have done nothing but tie the laces, completes the brand.

Among other reasons, companies brand in order to sell more product at a higher price. When Starbucks paints itself as more than a cup of coffee – like a comfortable spot playing trendy music where we can meet people – they can charge a premium for their coffee. Now we're paying for the experience surrounding the coffee, not just for the coffee itself.

Bedbury says that in today's world, to be successful, brands must understand deep psychological matters like "yearning to belong, needing to feel connected, hoping to transcend, desiring to experience joy and fulfillment."[14] It is not enough for companies to have their logos plastered everywhere; they also need to tap into our innate desires, the "hierarchy of needs"[15] placed inside us from the moment we were born. They know we are searching for meaning, and they are willing to help us find it – for a price.

A successful marketer attaches meaning to a product through advertising. For the marketer, industry devices such as spokespeople, music, events, and store design can be used to create meaning. At the same time, the marketer surveys existing pop-cultural expressions such as movies, novels, and fads and creates ways to associate the product with those ideas.

Through this process, marketers discover hot spots for consumers – the things, places, and people of cultural interest – and attach their products to them. Here the marketing magic takes on a surreal power. Somehow the product absorbs the meaning associated with these hot-spot pop-cultural expressions. To fit in and feel accepted, we buy the products perceived to have meanings that best express who we think we are, or who we want to be. Consciously or unconsciously, we believe our purchases define us.

On Sunday afternoon, when men turn on the football game – with all the running and hitting and memories of the glory days – testosterone flows. At the end of the quarter, the commercials start, and what do we see? Ads with pickup trucks running through creeks and over rocky terrain and carrying brawny things like steel and gravel; ads with pickup trucks towing other trucks and being dropped out of airplanes. Marketers design these ads to tap into a man's desire to feel manly. Men, wanting to look tough, desire a new truck. Meaning transfers.

To some extent, purchases can say something about us. We naturally buy certain products produced by certain brands depending on our hobbies and interests. It would be silly for pro surfer Chris Malloy to wear Ralph Lauren jeans and an Izod shirt. We would expect him to wear Hurley shorts and Patagonia shirts, clothes made for a certain type of person with certain types of interests. And so Chris Malloy conveys fragments of his personality every time he puts on his Patagonia flannel. This seems perfectly normal.

A problem arises, however, with our consumptive habits when we feel we have to buy certain items in order to gain personal meaning. When we begin manipulating our purchases, the issue then becomes one of motivation. Do we buy the Patagonia flannel because it is a natural expression of a personal aesthetic and functional preference? Or do we buy the shirt because we feel younger or cooler?

Consumption is not so much an action but an underlying belief system, a belief that personal meaning comes from the things we buy.

———

We have to live and work and purchase things. And though we know that a pair of shoes can't define us, we'd like to think they at least say *something* about us; and to some extent they do. But the shoes fade and wear out. We throw them away and look in the mirror – we're still there, still needing something the shoes couldn't give. Where do we find true meaning?

It's backward to think that our purchases can soothe the inner void we all feel. If this deep inner desire persists even when our purchases fade, then what we truly seek is not of this consumer world.

Intellectuals, for centuries, have sought to decipher the dual nature of human beings – our inner person consisting of a soul, and our outer person a fleshly body. The duality discussion pits the inner person against the outer person; one carries more worth than the other, depending on perspective.

The ancient Greeks, for example, regarded the body as a cage that kept the soul bound on earth, emphasizing the soul's importance. A physicalist (and some would argue an existentialist) emphasizes the interaction of the body within the world as primary to experiencing life. These views don't just appear without reason. The central questions they seek to answer relate to existence: Where do we come from? What constitutes a person?

The apostle Paul, though, treats the soul and body differently. He regards our bodies, or what the original language terms *soma*, as a unity of the inner person and the outer person—"the whole person as an entity before God."[16] So we, as human beings, aren't just composite parts. Our bodies and souls work in unison, from the inside out.

But when we focus our lives on an outward expression—consumption—seeking to produce inward meaning, we fragment ourselves. Even though we exist as whole beings, there's still a relational progression to encountering God (from the inside) and the world (outside). Since the need for meaning and identity is an inner need, we must address it by looking inward first. Ironically, a Christmas tree shows us this simple concept with clarity.

If you've ever cut your own tree or purchased a cut

tree, you know that a tree will hold its needles for only a certain amount of time. You can drill into the bottom of the tree and water it, but this will keep it flourishing for only so long. Eventually, the needles will turn brown and fall off. The sap will begin to run, and the tree will finally die. Then you'll take it out to the curb for the trash guys.

But what about that time in-between the tree being cut down and finally dying? We take it into our living room, stick it in a stand, and decorate it with ornaments and stars and knickknacks and tinsel and lights. We make it look as rich and beautiful as we can, only to throw it away a month later. Cutting a tree from its source of life and making it look good for a season, in the end, accomplishes little else than seasonal beauty.

It might seem silly to think of yourself as a Christmas tree, but is it that far-fetched? Away from our inner source (God), we can survive only for a time before we perish in the dry air of consumerism. The very things that make a Douglas fir beautiful are the color of its needles, the way the branches fall, its fragrance, its fruit (cones), and the texture of its bark. Cut the tree down and all that, eventually, goes away. It is the underground water supply that livens the tree's roots. The root system gives the tree its strength, the rich soil that holds the root ball together, nourishing and securing the trunk and limbs. The tree needs the underground source to make it beautiful to the world. Like *soma*—both parts working together, progressing from the inside (underground), out (the visible tree).

It's the same for humans. The very essence of our being comes from within. But when our sales receipts define us, we reduce ourselves to Christmas trees, beautiful on the outside, perched on our stands, while dying inside. We must not let our souls be martyred in exchange for the glitz of the immediate and temporal. For some of us, understandably, our root system scares us. Our inside feels mangled by our past mistakes and feelings of insecurity; these emotions confuse us, making it difficult to find our true selves. It's easier to put on our tinsel and garland and walk around looking good.

But whatever answers we are searching for won't be found in the emotional salve of a new car. No matter how much stuff we buy, we will still be left pining for meaning and significance. The slogans of an advertisement can't fully define us; they can't erase the moments of self-doubt; we need to feel loved and known for who we are.

———

We apply a little bit of veneer every time we purchase something to cover our feelings of doubt. Every day, we let someone else manipulate us into thinking we are not good enough, that we need something else, something special to set ourselves apart in order to prove our worth.

To search for meaning through a branded product image or the way that product makes us feel is to believe the carefully constructed lies of the consumer world. And if we continue to believe these lies, we will find our insides hollow.

"Watch out for people who try to dazzle you with big words and intellectual double-talk," warns Paul. "They want to drag you off into endless arguments that never amount to anything. They spread their ideas through the empty traditions of human beings and the empty superstitions of spirit beings. But that's not the way of Christ."[17] Paul cautions us to scrutinize the world's ideas and concepts.[18] The world inundates us with advertising and things to purchase, and if we are not careful, we will one day find ourselves neck deep in the clutter of our closet. Wisdom compels us to consider the implications of everything in this life, both spiritually and physically.

The tangible nature of our purchases gives us something to hold on to, something to measure others and ourselves with. They give us a sense of security that helps soothe our inner feelings of doubt. Again, this is false. "Nurtured in insecurity," writes theologian Edward Farley, "sin's motivation is to secure, to anchor human beings in a cosmos projected by itself, a creation of its own act of meaning or intentionality."[19]

We fool only ourselves in this scenario. Even though we think we are showing the world a version of ourselves through our purchases, in the long run, those closest to us see past our outer expressions. Eventually, self-reflection and close relationships lead us to the truth about ourselves.[20]

When we were created in his image, God made us whole. And so we start our quest for meaning with our relationship to him. Only then will we find satisfaction. God invites us into relationship with him, and if we accept, we will echo God's intention for us.[21] We will find meaning.

By scrutinizing the motivation of our purchases (and limiting them), we allow ourselves space to breathe, space enough to hear the whisperings of God. And through realigning our spiritual lives, we are able to transcend the cultural fragments of the advertising world that blitz us daily.

If pressed, most of us would admit that pursuing the materialism of the world doesn't make us a complete person. But how many of us are willing to live this way? How many of us are willing to forsake this world of things for God? As we pursue a deeper relationship with him, we are able to see the manipulation of this finite world burn away and our soul begin to sprout. And there, within our soul, we find the source of our meaning and purpose. Paul counted everything as "worthless when compared with the infinite value of knowing Christ Jesus."[22]

Chapter Four

THE GREAT VANISHING

Wrestling with Progress

Now the air I tasted and breathed
has taken a turn.

— *Pearl Jam, "Black"*

The buzz of the alarm clock shoves you out of bed and you stumble toward the kitchen to start the coffee brewing. With sleep still covering your eyes, you fumble around grinding the beans and running the water. You turn toward the coffeemaker and *poof*, it vanishes. "What the …!" you shriek as you jump back a couple of feet. You swivel your head around and see everything vanishing in a blink. You grab your iPhone to call someone – *poof*, gone. Then the flat screen, gone. One by one, the laptop, Xbox, iPad all vanish.

You run to your bedroom to throw on some clothes and get out of the house. As soon as you kick the closet door open, things start vanishing. Your jeans, your new Nikes, the cashmere sweater you bought on sale last week – gone. Screaming, you grab your keys off the dresser and run out the door – *poof*, the Volkswagen, gone. You run over to where the car sat two seconds earlier and slowly look around the neighborhood. "What's going on?" you ask yourself.

You take a couple of deep breaths to calm yourself and count to five. Then you walk back inside and plop onto the couch in disbelief. Sitting there, contemplating your next move, a gust of wind hits you in the face and *swoosh*, your flat screen is back. You jump off the couch, *swoosh*, your iPhone's back. Coffeemaker, jeans, sweater all pop back into place.

It's odd to imagine things – our possessions, our tools, our materials – appearing and disappearing and reappearing. But this story represents an exaggerated view of what a true consumer society could look like. We labor each day so we can earn enough money to buy things. Things that will break and be thrown away, that will disappear. Once gone, we buy them again and they reappear. This is our shiny-disposable-things world.

Eventually we become numb to that type of world and we plod along through life trying to buy and sell our way to a happy existence. Political theorist Hannah Arendt warns of a society that becomes blind and numb from consuming. "[If] we were truly nothing but members of a consumers' society," she writes in her book *The Human Condition*, "we would no longer live in a world at all but simply be driven by a process in whose ever-recurring cycles things appear and disappear, manifest themselves and vanish, never to last long enough to surround the life process in their midst."[1]

What Arendt describes sounds much like today's world, where technology constantly collides with consumption.

The collision cycle drives us: we work in order to consume, the more we consume the more we must produce. Produce. Consume. Produce. Consume. Arendt further cautions that such a society will, eventually, be unable to see its own futility.

Technology, in the form of industrial progress and computer technology, becomes a driving factor in a veneered world acting as a consumption amplifier. Streamlined manufacturing processes enable companies to produce items at breakneck speeds. Innovations in materials create products that may not last forever but seem affordable. Shipping logistics make it possible to produce goods almost anywhere in the world capitalizing on cheap labor, driving prices lower.

The internet amplifies our consuming further, allowing us to buy a seemingly infinite amount of goods with the click of a button. We can sit on our couch in Idaho, visit the website of a company in California, and buy a phone that was assembled in China with parts made in Malaysia. We browse for shoes and books and electronics and, with "one click," our purchase arrives on our doorstep the next day. As kings and queens of our consumer world, we can buy things whenever we want, and this doesn't bother us one bit; it's convenient.

Theologian Philip Sampson warns of a serious consequence in a world where purchases give us meaning and progress allows for the massive production of goods: "once established, such a culture of consumption is quite undiscriminating and everything becomes a consumer item." It seems we've become *quite* undiscriminating.

Mark Zuckerberg was only nineteen when he created the now-monstrous website Facebook. In its first seven years, the site boasts 550 million members who, collectively, spend 700 billion minutes each month reading wall posts and updating statuses. Membership to Facebook grows by 700,000 new users a day. If Facebook were a country, it would be the third largest in the world.[2] And the aggressive growth of the site is not without a reason; the idea of connecting people seems brilliant – find an old friend from elementary school, or stay in touch with cousins you normally see only at Christmas, or keep your family up to date on the thrills of college life. Most of us love connectivity. On some level, we feel that we are staying in touch with all 892 of our friends.

But as great as this seems, a downside emerges. Like the rest of the internet, Facebook allows us to browse. But instead of browsing news reports or items to fill our shopping cart, we're browsing people. We look up a friend to see what they are doing, where they work or vacation or live. We read snippets about their lives and move on. We search through our friends, choosing which ones to check on and interact with, much like we would a Google search. And no matter how we try to spin it, commenting on someone's wall is not the same as interacting with them in person. We could call it social consumption.

In 2010, *Time* magazine honored Zuckerberg with its Person of the Year award, a distinction held by notable figures like Winston Churchill, Martin Luther King Jr., and Ronald Reagan. In his profile of Zuckerberg, reporter Lev Grossman points out that Facebook "smooshes together your work self and your home self, your past self and your present self, into a single generic extruded product."

We live in an age when the complexity of humanity can compress itself into byte-sized chunks of ones and zeros – our hobbies, interests, and religious views all relegated to what can fit into a form on a website, our relationship status reduced to the choices offered by a drop-down menu, our opinions synthesized to 140 characters. Jaron Lanier, computer scientist and author, writes that "a new generation has come of age with a reduced expectation of what a person can be."[3]

In the comic strip *Calvin and Hobbes*, young Calvin, a six-year-old with a vivid imagination, takes a cardboard box, writes "Transmogrifier" on the outside, climbs inside, and emerges as a space creature or dinosaur or whatever he wants to be. It's one of Calvin's favorite games. It's the game we now play with technology; we climb into our computers only to resurface as avatars, status updates, and homemade celebrities.

The collision between consumption and technology has a startling aftereffect that burns past the endless supply of consumable products. We have, in essence, altered the reality of the human race. Not only do we see technology acting as a consumption amplifier, we see a second trait start to emerge: humanity transmogrifier.

In the *New York Times*, Sherry Turkle, a psychologist and the director of the M.I.T. Initiative on Technology and Self, was quoted as saying that when we're on the computer, on our networks in Facebook, "we are no longer able to distinguish when we are together and nurtured and when we are alone and isolated. I can be in intimate contact with 300 people on e-mail, but when I look up from my computer I feel bereft. I haven't heard a voice, touched a hand, for hours or days. I think people are no longer certain where the self resides."[4]

From our couch, we fade into the invisible, people devoid of tangible interaction, our real actions glossed over with pithier status updates, our pictures self-curated, our wall-posts filled with trite comments. We miss the nuance, the intricacy, and the beauty of real, in-person social interaction. In the end, the web offers only feel-good shots of experience. We've fallen asleep in the land of handshakes and eye contact and walks on the beach and awakened in a world where humans look like products in an online shopping cart—downloadable, browse-able, clickable, even deleteable.

More than ever, we *feel* connected with each other. But browsing data does not produce relationships. Our lives become strewn about the web. Fragmented. People encounter online life-widgets, but they don't see the grit; they see only the facade we hoist up for all to see. Our life story, a mini-wiki page: bookmarked, filed, accumulated. Our avatars and profiles look like splinters of who we really are. At the end of the day, we can close our relationships as we close our laptops, untouched and unmoved by the lives of others. But life is not like that. It's rich with nuance and complexity. It is unrelenting and never shuts off, a concurrence of the terrible and beautiful.

From the Christian perspective, life is about the here and now, real people living real lives in a real world. Created beings set forth in the cosmos to create societies, families, and to reflect the glory of God, we live and die in this real world. But we also look to something beyond the here and now. Rooted in the reality of now, we are catapulted forward by our anticipation of being reunited with our Father God. Life, then, looks like a beautiful mixture of the real world that we encounter with our senses and the world we cannot see – that place of unapproachable light where God resides. This blend of the real and the transcendent places a certain kind of specialness on each human being. It places us above the brute animals in that we are self-conscious, we have unique personalities, we have the capacity to love and be loved, we can relate to God. For God weaves every person together in the waiting room of real life; we are "fearfully and wonderfully made," each of us mysteriously living with the ability to reach toward eternity yet frustrated in our efforts because we are finite.

So we exist in a healthy tension between heaven and earth. But at times it seems like humans are determined to erase any uniqueness or specialness from our race. We are now a generation linked to the Facebook understanding of human interaction – "generic extruded products." And no matter how well we defend the great ways to connect through this digital medium, we know, in our heart of hearts, that something is amiss. As we power up the computer and browse our friends just before bed, we know that the feeling we receive in our gut isn't a feeling of relational peace. It is, rather, an understanding that all our online friendships cannot equal one real person sitting next to us listening to our life story, empathizing with our hurt, embracing our body, and just "being" there for us.

It's no surprise that so many of us run to Facebook

and other social sites. The longing for closeness weaves throughout the fabric of our very being. But collecting digital profiles isn't a shortcut to real relationships.

The world of social consumption has led us down an unthinkable path to a place that values a thing more than a human. In his *Discourse on Metaphysics*, philosopher G. W. Leibniz says that "no matter how precious it [a thing] is," we should value humans above all else. He points readers to the relationship that humans have with God and observes that "the greatest satisfaction that a soul ... can have is to see itself loved by others."[5]

You have a lunch meeting with eight of your associates. You know them all well enough. The lunch gathering is actually a send-off lunch for one of your friends, who just resigned. Of the eight people sitting at the table, you are the only one who does not have an iPhone. You know this because everyone is looking at their phones, feigning busyness.

The waitress brings the rolls and everyone digs in — slurps of drinks, slathering of butter. But no one really knows how to start up conversation. Everyone chows down while exchanging uncomfortable glances. You squirm in the awkwardness, knifing through the tension.

So to break up the weirdness, you stir up some conversation. "Well, what are your plans? You have a plan ... right?"

"Oh, yeah. I have guaranteed work for three months at this other firm. After that, we'll see."

Small conversations about nothing spring up. You're on your third glass of lemon water.

"More lemon, please."

You make another attempt at a conversation, but this time you're greeted by "the gesture." We're all familiar with the gesture: another person reaching for his or her phone to check something at the same time you are talking.

You're too late. Whatever you are saying cannot compete with the three-inch screen of a phone. Your mind goes into hyperdrive as you think through what you would love to say. "No! Look. I'm right here. Be *here*! What could you possibly be checking? The whole firm is right here. Look at *us*. Talk to *us*. If you want to tap something, tap my shoulder or tap your fourth glass of lemon water."

You feel yourself teetering on the brink of social insanity; as you pan the table, almost everyone is checking their phones again. Emails. Texts. Weather reports. Videos. Word docs. PDFs. Games. All these wonderful digital things appear more important than the live human being sitting right there across the table in a chair, sucking on lemon water.

Our society is like a microwave. We push the short-cut buttons to warm our lives, buy stuff we don't need, and ignore our friends. Ding! Our TV-dinner life is ready. Maybe the new smartphone will have an app for happiness.

Perhaps this seems like an overstatement of the problem. But this scenario is based on real events. We've all had our conversations interrupted by the head dip, checking email or a text message. It's not enough that we are ebbing away into the invisible world via social networking; now the virtual world entices us more than a live person.

Without noticing, we have started to drift from one another to the point that even in the presence of friends, we would rather hide in our invisible worlds. We try to disappear so we don't have to endure the aching nuisance of live interaction.

But we *are* real. We are not invisible. We have a nose and fingertips. We have eyes that see things and minds to contemplate it all. We physically interact with our surroundings. The world is a tactile place, not merely to be experienced but to be encountered.

And yet we do everything in our power to isolate ourselves from each other. We shop, online. We bank, online. We foster relationships, online. We do our best to digitize our existence. There is, however, a cultural reaction to a world where everything exists in the virtual. We see this reaction played out in movies such as *The Matrix*, *Gattaca*, *V for Vendetta*, and *Fight Club*.

In *Fight Club*, Edward Norton plays a nonchalant and timid man (and the narrator) who subconsciously creates Tyler Durden – the make-believe alter ego of Norton's character. Tyler is an anarchist, bloodthirsty, violence-crazed sex freak who gets his thrills by getting beat up. Together they create a black-market, underground cult dubbed "Fight Club." The club exists without the big lights, the crowds, and the women. It happens in basements across the nation where numb men gather to feel again. Bare-knuckled and driven to rage, these guys bludgeon one another in friendly sparring matches, all in the name of "feeling alive" – of feeling, period.[6]

Fight Club members are sworn to secrecy and create a massive brotherhood given to senseless vandalism aimed at "big money," "big corporations," and anything in general that saps them of their humanity. Many of the men are social rejects or corporate nobodies (like Norton's character) who feel they are wasting away, emasculated by a society bent on keeping all humans in cubicles attached to their plastic cards and lattes.

Fight Club's message projects with clarity: people desperately want to feel and be part of something that celebrates their identity; people harbor a deep resentment toward the things that cause them not to feel; people crave attention from someone or something and will go to any lengths to get it.

But it seems, given the chance, we would rather throw ourselves into a transmogrifier just to escape from the mundane. Why? What is it about the real that frightens us so?

Westley, in the film *The Princess Bride*, enlightens Princess Buttercup to the realities of this world when he rebuts her "woe is me, my pain is so great" rant with a resounding "life *is* pain ... anyone who says different is selling you something."

Westley is right. Life is pain. And pain deepens us. It often feels like an iron digging into our souls, chipping away the shale of our hearts, and delivering massive blows to our egos and pride. Slowly the hole inside of us opens, crumbling on all sides, the bottom a loose mess of clay and gravel.

The iron pries and twists until we no longer resemble the same earthen vessel we used to be. We have become an open wound, a scar of the earth primed for planting—loam able to sustain a living organism. In this metamorphosis, we see how pain shapes us into people who are able to take on the constant churning of life. We see that with love and relationships comes a richness that pain can help form. The fruit that pain produces nourishes us; the fruit of memories, the fruit of blessings, the fruit of struggle and triumph feed us and make us even more fertile.

This new abundance has come from the swinging iron, from the thrusting shovel, from the toil and care of the One who works the soil to produce beneficial fruit. We can hide behind our computer screen avoiding hurt and loss and the *real* as much as we want, but in the end we will miss out on the essence of life.

Perhaps we would rather fade away into the invisible because we can control our virtual existence. But our online experiences and relationships offer only a fraction of the beauty and complexity that fill our real lives. How wonderful is the great technological world. And yet how much more wonderful and deep and beautiful is our real world. Unlike our computers, life can't be shut down.

Chapter Five

OH, INVERTED WORLD

Understanding Society

IT MIGHT SOUND BORING,
BUT IT'S THE BORING STUFF
I REMEMBER THE MOST.

– *Russell,* Up

"Good evening," says Mr. Howard K. Smith, journalist and moderator of the debate. "The television and radio stations of the United States and their affiliated stations are proud to provide facilities for a discussion of issues in the current political campaign by the two major candidates for the presidency."*

It's 1960 and television is new to political debate.

"And now for the first opening statement by Senator John F. Kennedy," Mr. Smith says, cueing the opening statements.

"I'm not satisfied when I see men like Jimmy Hoffa – in charge of the largest union in the United States – still free. I'm not satisfied when we are failing to develop the natural resources of the United States to the fullest." Kennedy is handsome and approachable, his words and demeanor confident, trusting.

The camera cuts to Nixon. He is older and looks it. He comes across as an edgy stoic, gruff. "Let us understand," he implores, "throughout this campaign that his motives and mine are sincere. I know what it means to be poor. I know what it means to see people who are unemployed. I know Senator Kennedy feels as deeply about these problems as I do, but our disagreement is not about the goals for America but only about the means to reach those goals."

Nixon versus Kennedy. Nixon was the seasoned veteran; he had spent eight years as vice president under Eisenhower. Kennedy, the son of an Irish businessman and politician, was the up and comer from Boston. Neither side knew how their candidate would fare in the new format, but as the cameras rolled and the debate continued, the differences in their personalities and styles became exaggerated. Under the bright lights, the vice president looked nervous as sweat beaded on his head, and the camera accentuated his pale skin and five o'clock shadow.

In contrast, Kennedy looked tan, calm, and collected. His classic good looks agreed with the camera, and regardless of the candidates' answers, Nixon appeared disheveled while Kennedy seemed to have things under control.[1] The people of America were watching politics change as on-camera presence became just as important as policy. A full head of hair, a smooth speaking voice, an appearance not too old but not too young—looks and on-screen performance meant something when being broadcast to an entire nation.

———

In *Politics*, Aristotle wrote that "what the statesman is most anxious to produce is a certain moral character in his fellow citizens, namely a disposition to virtue and the performance of virtuous actions."[2] In modern politics, however, politicians look more like celebrities than statesman. Strong policies and virtuous action have been replaced with five-hundred-dollar haircuts and winning smiles. News programs run short biographical pieces on their lives so that we can get to "know them" just like the other celebrities we follow. They appear on *The View* and *Letterman* and *Saturday Night Live*. The front pages of the tabloids speculate about their workout routines and showcase the designer clothes of their spouses and children.

More than celebrities, the politicians are ad men too. Easy-to-remember sound bites, fit for an advertising campaign, become headlines in the morning papers. Polling data and focus groups provide the campaign with clues as to what we, the people, want to hear. And like the great advertisers of the world, politicians mix up truth with fabrication to spin reality in a new way. In hopes of being elected, they routinely manipulate the truth and cover over facts. In the final debate of the 2008 presidential election, the *Washington Post* found a total of fifteen misrepresentations of the truth between the two candidates.[3]

This misrepresentation of the truth epitomizes the problem of a society covered with veneer. Nothing seems real. The fake feels real, and so the real seems unbelievable. All of society looks upside-down. And with no bearing, we stumble along in a counterfeit world where all of society wants to project its own version of the real.

We see a skewed version of reality in our nation's education system. The federal No Child Left Behind law mandates that states bring 100 percent of their students to the states' proficiency level in math and reading. Each state sets its own academic standards and then tests students to measure proficiencies against those standards. However, a study by the Department of Education showed that fifteen states across the country lowered their academic standards. This move allows students to test lower than previous years but still appear to be testing high. To the average parent or outsider, it seems the students are progressing, but in reality, they aren't performing any higher. "At a time when we should be raising standards to compete in the global economy, more states are lowering the bar than raising it,"

Secretary of Education Arne Duncan said in a statement. "We're lying to our children."[4]

It should come as no surprise that the entertainment industry portrays a version of reality that differs from the truth. Take pop singer Katy Perry. Her record label marketed her as a sultry sexpot. It worked. Her 2009 release, *One of the Boys*, has sold more than seven million copies worldwide. Her 2010 album, *Teenage Dream*, debuted at number one on the Billboard charts and received a Grammy nomination for album of the year. In 2001, she had released an album on a Christian record label under her given name, Katy Hudson. That one didn't do so well. For the sake of sales, for marketing, her new label veneered her name, her image, and her music to make a product provocative enough for your seventeen-year-old daughters and impressionable teenage sons to buy.

Businesses regularly bend reality far past the reach of an ad campaign. In the 1920s, America's highways were filled with cars that were built to last a lifetime and all looked the same. Since you might buy only one car in your entire life, outselling market-leader Ford was a tough task for competitor General Motors.

General Motors eventually realized, though, that they could create a demand for new cars, even if your existing car ran fine, by giving buyers color options and changing those options every year. At the same time, they started focusing on how the car looked—the style, the lines, the curves of the body.

Prior to this, manufacturers worried only about quality. Henry Ford, with only one model of car at the time, once remarked that customers could get a car in any color they wanted, as long as it was black. General Motors made style important, which dated cars, and so they created a market for new models. They built their cars to wear out so consumers would need to replace them and, even if your car ran fine, you might still *trade up* if it appeared outdated. General Motors created demand where it previously did not exist.

Fast-forward to today, and cars are still marketed in this way.[5] This false demand created by obsolescence of style, along with a planned obsolescence in which things are built to break, has become a major strategy for most businesses.

Television distorts reality with every click of the remote. In 2010 the final episode of MTV's reality show *The Hills* surprised viewers. Two cast members, Brody and Kristen, were saying goodbye to each other as Kristen was leaving for Europe. The two had been dating on and off since the show began, and this seemed like the end of their relationship. They hugged and Brody helped Kristen into her car. As the car drove off and Brody stood watching, a series of clips from past episodes played.

The clips highlighted the emotion of the moment by recapping the long history of the couple. As the montage ended, Brody stared off into the distance as the camera panned out, revealing additional cameras and backdrops and a production crew. The scene was filmed on a studio lot.

For six seasons viewers had been watching the show, and now they were left wondering whether it had been real or fake. Or whether it had been a little bit of both. Had *The Hills* been cast and scripted just like other shows on television?

As much as we may like to believe that reality shows are real, they've never have had much reality to them. They may use real people instead of actors and real houses instead of sets, but once a camera crew invades someone's life, reality changes. The editors control what we see, presenting episodes with various degrees of dramatic tension or comedic relief.

This manufactured reality plays out on the newsstands, where magazines sell us their version of reality every day: they Photoshop the women on their covers to digital perfection, selling it as beauty. Wrinkles removed, breasts enlarged, thighs tightened, legs elongated – women are airbrushed into a reality that doesn't exist. It can't exist. So women readers are sold a false version of reality that leaves them feeling awkward and ashamed, and men are given a rendering of a woman that they will never find.

As a result of all of this reality-bending seen throughout society, we end up stuck inside a gray-colored middle world, somewhere between the real and the false. When we reach for the real, we find that it doesn't compare to the expectations set by the society around us. Women can't compete with the sex-crazed TV wife. Men can't compete with the buff TV husband who always knows what to say. We can't compete because what the media presents isn't real.

The boring. The mundane. The rhythms of life. These are the things that make for awful politics, bad business, and terrible television. Society doesn't do so well when dealing with reality. It's tough to gain power and control and wealth without rubbing a little of the truth off of things.

But if you turn off the TV, close the magazines, and look up, you will find a very real world. A world where we don't always have the right answers, a world where we blunder with awkward pauses and embarrassing slipups, a world where we put on weight and lose our hair and grow old. In the real world, the daily grind can't be ignored. You have to tie your shoes and clip your toenails and take out the trash. Like Russell, the chubby Wilderness Explorer from the movie *Up*, says, "It's the boring stuff I remember the most."

———

"He is not a god you can trust!" The words are more growled than spoken.

"But what if he ..."

"He won't. And if he does, we'll be ready for him."

The uneasy crowd exchanges looks. Some are buying the bit, others stand in fear, while still others are vehement and crazed.

"Look what we've created. We did this," shouts another would-be leader. "We prospered on our own. We don't need anyone's blessing to be great. We *are* great."

And with that they began to build. Upward, skyward went their defiance in the form of a tower, in the form of a temple. Led in anger and fear, the people gathered in their arrogance and in their self-made glory to show God that they could be gods too, that they *were* gods too.

Babel stood as center stage for that culture to take a bow, to itself. It was the place where all the races of man gathered to revel in their own accomplishments. They knew they could be great without God, and they wanted to prove it.[6]

In a veneered society, the people of Shinar should sound familiar to us. Our society may not be building a massive tower toward the sky, but we do raise ourselves up as human towers in our accomplishments. We stand in the shadow of our pride, look around at all the things our hands and minds have made, and we can't help but think that we don't need God for anything. Look what we can do on our own.

Babel represents a society that sees through the monocle of self. It stands in awe of its cultural trinkets, thinking that somehow all they created will give that society meaning and purpose. But they created in isolation from God, elevating the self as greater than God. As we progress and our processes and innovations become greater, man becomes less dependent on God. And here we see that veneer in society not only distorts reality but also creates a false sense of accomplishment. We can achieve whatever we want, and so we veneer over our need for a God.

We think that the progress of society somehow means better — better me, better you, better job. But even with all that society can accomplish, we can't seem to solve the big problems facing humanity. We can genetically modify seeds to produce endless amounts of corn, yet people still die of hunger every day. We can harvest stem cells and perform embryonic research, but disease continues to ravage humanity. We can connect with anyone on the planet, but we still suffer from depression and loneliness. We can amass billions of dollars, yet our cities swell with the homeless and impoverished. People still murder and get sick and leave their spouses. Society could build a tower that reaches the moon if it wanted, but it will never mend all the broken pieces of the human race.

Poet-monk Thomas Merton, in his book *The New Man*, describes man's intended relationship to God: "Man resembles God in so far as he too, like God, is a worker, a ruler, a creator, and a father." As we attend to the business of running the world, we are in effect invoking God's image and likeness as imitators of him. Of course, this is the ideal situation: all of us seeking to imitate God in all we do as we govern and teach and build the world, using our creativity and power to bring glory to God. But humankind shuns God, and his creativity often becomes self-serving. Merton concludes, "When we rail against God with our progress and advancement for our own glory our society becomes geared not only against God, but against the most fundamental natural interests of man himself."[7]

When we have a society that works to elevate man and his desires over what God desires and has no sense of what is real or false, our sense of morality fractures. Society beats our very humanity down to the point where we orient ourselves not toward God but toward the desires of the whole of society, the mob.

———

The mob man looks to satisfy his carnality with greed, illicit sex, and violence. Open a magazine or turn on the television or go to the movies; the themes seen over and over again revolve around one, or all three, of these. It doesn't take too keen of an observer to notice the immorality rampant in our society.

In 2009 a San Francisco school made headlines when a fifteen-year-old girl was gang raped in an alley at a school-sanctioned dance. At least twenty people were involved in the two-and-a-half-hour ordeal, either by watching or participating in the act. The girl was found hours later, unconscious beneath a bench.[8]

This story appalls us. It breaks our hearts: a fifteen-year-old girl, gang raped — at her school. We read this story in the paper and we want justice. But how upset can we be? Our films, our music, our books are filled with violence and sex. Rape, murder, and corporate scandal — this is exactly the kind of behavior we should expect to see in a society that celebrates the profane.

In 2008 Rapper Lil Wayne released his album *Tha Carter III*. The album has sold more than 3.5 million copies worldwide, garning much critical acclaim and a Grammy Award. Explicit lyrics litter the album, focusing on sex, money, and violence. We shouldn't find it shocking that our society produces young men who gang rape a fifteen-year-old; after all, millions of young men buy Lil Wayne albums.

Who's to blame for this? Lil Wayne, and others like him in music and television and film? If people weren't buying this type of entertainment or giving out awards for it or profiting from it, then, arguably, the industry would produce something else. But in the pursuit of profits, companies will do anything they can to make more money. They fabricate reality and pander to our carnal desires. They use deep-seated wickedness as a marketing gimmick. Like singer-songwriter David Bazan says, "If it isn't making dollars, then it isn't making sense."[9]

Artifacts of the profane fill pop culture. We watch a crime show and routinely see someone being bludgeoned to death. We turn on a music awards show and see a singer dancing half-naked on stage while men and women emulate sex acts in the background. We open a fashion magazine and find half-dressed men and women. We open the Sunday paper and read about a CEO extorting money or heading up a Ponzi scheme.

In such a society, actions once shocking to us, actions that our parents scoffed at, are now common. Madonna dances on stage, and we are outraged. Twenty years later, she does it again and it's no big deal. Everything has to be "one-upped" in order to stand out, or it just becomes expected. If one crime drama shows a man beaten to death, another show will have a man beaten to death by two men in a strip club.

And people want the sex and violence and greed. These things make for entertaining television and for music we can dance to. They become like drugs; the high we once experienced fades and we need a greater high. We need more egregious sex or violence.

So the desires of the mob man take control, bending the whole of the society toward an average. As individuals, our morals twist toward those of the masses. We stop questioning the things we once questioned as the rest of the world slowly pulls us along. That which makes us a person – our individuality – fades, and in exchange, we consume mass-produced entertainment meant to appeal to society's lowest common denominator. Jacques Ellul talks about this idea in his book *Propaganda*. He writes, "The individual never is considered as an individual, but always in terms of what he has in common with others, such as his motivations, his feelings, or his myths. He is reduced to an average."[10]

The veneered world excludes the individual. The individual is hard to market to, hard to convince. If society had to consider unique individuals, it would lack any real influence. Society derives its power from the masses – the power to distort and to corrupt and to persuade. It has the power to steal our fundamental belief systems from us and replace them with the belief systems of the mob man.

But we are not an average; we are not part of a trend. We are created individuals, unique creatures with our own tastes and preferences, likes and dislikes. We were meant to have a personality. We were not meant to be part of an average. We were not meant to live in a hijacked land, but "man in his self-seeking defiance has given himself over to the dominion of alien lords and tyrants"[11] and seems content to roam the earth faceless, heartless – soulless.

When we look at society as a whole, we cannot help but feel overcome by an immense sadness. We, the human race, have fallen captive to a world that paints every person in the same color, the same frame. And devoid of our individuality, we sink into isolation – from each other and from God.[12]

⸻

Along with the societal influences of politics, business, entertainment, media, and other social expressions, we find the church. Since the church's inception in Acts 2, its identity has ebbed and flowed in many expressions throughout history. From persecuted subsect of Judaism to dominant

Roman Catholicism to sixteenth-century Protestantism, the church always seemed to know when it needed a revival. Church scholar Bruce Winter suggests that the church endures a reformation every four hundred years. If that's the case, we're about due.

The church, as a social institution, must also deal with cultural shifts in knowledge, meaning, and language. From its inception, the church was never static in its proclamation of God's Word; the church constantly searches for ways to engage the world with the gospel. But as the church accepts the norms of society, its message can be compromised for the sake of relevance. As a result, the church begins to resemble society – using its success metrics, getting caught under the same types of veneers. It's one thing to understand the felt needs of those who are hearing the gospel message but quite another to diminish the actual message, which is what happens when the church applies the veneers of society.

In an attempt to adapt to society, the twenty-first-century evangelical church is undergoing changes of its own. From home church to simple church to deep church to emerging church to online church to incarnational-missional church, the church's buzzword lexicon grows exponentially with each new church-growth conference. The relevant seeker-sensitive model, however, seems to influence most new churches. This well-intentioned model uses many of the same techniques found in magazines and malls and arenas across the country. This church boasts "experience architects" and "producers" and "creative directors" who manufacture environments where the attendee can "experience God."

God, however, is not a sideshow. He does not reside in some Gothic temple awaiting our visit so that we can experience him and move on with life. He is Spirit, a trinity, who cannot be manipulated into space and time, a being to encounter, know, and worship.

But what do we mean by worship?

As a society, we have come to expect a certain level of production quality when we listen to music or watch movies or television. As a church, with technology and proper financial resources, the professionalism found in these forms of entertainment can be mimicked and thus meet the expectations of congregants. This is why some of the biggest and most modern churches the world over boast enormous production budgets, complete with professional musicians and sound technicians.

If we back up and look at the Christian landscape with as much objectivity as possible, we can't help but notice how much society influences the church. From building architecture to worship style, the relevant church takes its cues from the Apples and Starbucks and U2s of the world.

We've successfully bottled God with a neat worship funnel. By the time song five gets pumping, the audience knows what to expect. This kind of predictability marks our society — the seeking of the sensory so we can feel more. Unfortunately, many churches don't offer an alternative to these expectations; they capitalize on them.

When you stand in the middle of two thousand people and the smoke is lifting with the lights and the guitar delay reverberates through the auditorium, you would be dead if you weren't taken up by the experience. Your heart pounds, vocals soar. You see the worship leader on the nine-hundred-square-foot high-definition screen — cut to close up of hands on guitar — and become entranced. All your senses fire your emotions. It's overwhelming.

When we spend less than 2 percent of our week at church, it's odd to think our time together should mimic what we experience every one of the previous six days. It should be two hours of the total *other*. It should be a break from the norm. The most perplexing presupposition of it all is thinking that the outside world wants the church to look exactly like the same thing they get at the mall.

Leading the way for the church, we find the pastor.[13] In part, the position of pastor seems to be tainted by celebrity culture. The pages of Christian magazines are covered with "hot" new pastors and whatever message they're preaching at the time. They amass followers on Twitter, fans on Facebook, and they make short videos in which they star in the lead role. Sadly, if a pastor stumbles, his story becomes front-page news. In a society that praises celebrities, we find it natural to "celebrate the extraordinary minister more than the ordinary ministry of the gospel."[14]

Traditionally, the pastor's role was defined as a shepherd. Peter instructs the church leadership to "care for God's flock with all the diligence of a shepherd."[15] Today, the role is more entrepreneur and marketer. The skill set of the traditional pastor and the modern pastor could not be more different. A shepherd-pastor's chief concern is his flock, to disciple and care for it. An entrepreneur-pastor's chief concern is his product (brand) and results. He must play by the rules of the marketplace: consumer demand, growth, profits and losses, return on investment. When a marketing genius runs a church, the way the church operates – the church building and methodology – will resemble his leadership style. Pastor and scholar John Piper laments, "We have, by and large, lost the biblical vision of a pastor as one who is mighty in the Scriptures, apt to teach, competent to confute opponents, and able to penetrate to the unity of the whole counsel of God."[16]

We aren't, however, the first to deal with the issue of popularity in the church. Indeed, the Corinthian church existed in a society filled with cults, idol worship, intellectual elitism, and temple prostitution – a culture of luxury and sexual laxity.[17] The Corinthian church wanted what was relevant to the culture, a great orator to wow them: "the Corinthians were enamored with sophistry, teachers of rhetoric were in high demand in this city where movers and shakers had a better chance at upward mobility than in older, well-established cities built on bedrock traditions. This is why Paul spends the first four chapters of 1 Corinthians demoting the art of public speaking and promoting the power of a gospel that exalts the weak and the foolish."[18]

Paul turns this kind of culture on its ear, instructing the church to serve "people without respect for their persona and their usefulness or any personal political aspirations typical of patronage." Apparently Paul's warning to the Corinthians worked. Christians and the church "were no longer the fawning and flattering parasites of private patrons," writes New Testament theologian Bruce Winter, "subservient to their ambitions and daily agendas, but they were family – the family of God."[19]

If anything, the church of Corinth reminds us that hooking on to the popular culture can have disastrous results for the gospel. Focusing on the outward gifts of men and women and giving them popular preferential treatment because they somehow "measure up" better than others is antithetical to the values inherent in the family of God. If the cultural language speaks in contradiction to the message of Christ, then we not only have to evaluate it and weigh all our decisions corporately, methodologically, and spiritually, but we also need the courage to counter the culture.

———

In a small article on church trends, pastor Francis Chan explains what he did when he set out to start his church in Simi Valley, California. He simply looked around at what other successful pastors were doing and followed suit. He mentions that it didn't dawn on him to perhaps consult Scripture and pray about what it means to *be* the church. Chan's honesty serves as an example to us all. Are we merely following what others are doing, or are we seeking God's will for his family? Are we building Towers of Babel with our churches, or do we gather to get on our faces before God?[20]

Methods of sharing God's love with all of humanity need to breathe with the changing times. But society and the church can go too far. The early church's stance on the Greco-Roman theater was not to attend, because of rampant immorality. Luther's stance on justification through faith flew in the face of the Catholic Church. These examples show that it's possible and appropriate for the church not to coalesce with the popular norms of society and still thrive. Just because the rest of society does something popular, or certain churches use so-called innovative methods to spur growth, doesn't make it right. We forget that worldly success seldom mirrors godly success. Often they are opposed.

What would happen if we started to view ourselves — the called-out ones — less as an institutional organization and more as a family, less as a cultural expression and more as a brother-sister co-op of redeemed sinners passionate about God? Would this change anything in how society perceives the church?

The church, as the family of God, represents God's answer to a world that has lost itself under its veneer — a way *to be* before God and to the world. It stands as an otherworldly alternative to a society in need of the rich blessings stemming from a family built on endless grace.

Unfortunately, when we see the church only through the lens of society, we end up reducing it to fit into a cultural structure. "So many who understand themselves to be followers of Jesus," writes Eugene Peterson, "without hesitation, and apparently without thinking, embrace the ways and means of the culture as they go about their daily living 'in Jesus' name.' "[21]

And so the modern family of God finds itself in a dilemma. The church wants to be this organic relational thing, yet measure success by the world's definition. "In our society growth equals success," says Scott Thumma in *Forbes* magazine, "... and religious growth not only equals success but also God's blessing on the ministry."[22] The church, then, exists in a tension that gives way to concession. After all, we were called to success. Right?

But the ways society measures success differ from the ways in which Jesus leads us.[23] As the family of God, we should consider an alternative. And when we reflect on how we as individuals and as a family relate to God the Father, Jesus the Son, and the Holy Ghost, we remember that our lives begin at Jesus' death. We realize that the ways of the world — the veneer — pale when we see ourselves rightly related to him, when we see ourselves through the lens of redemption.

AN ETHEREAL PLANE

The Language of God

AND AFTER THE FIRE CAME A GENTLE WHISPER.

— 1 Kings 19:12 NIV

The beauty of the fall morning catches you by surprise as you open the front door. The sun, not quite awake, offers a faint light through the rising fog. "With all those East Coast leaves floating around like embers from burning trees,"[1] you climb into your car, off to meet friends for an early coffee. Driving the back roads, you see more than the blurring oak trees lining the road. In the rearview mirror, you see a strange beacon blaring through the boughs of the trees, creating an ethereal flickering. The bouncing light hits your squinting eyes, and you look away. Then you look again. You wonder what is happening and sense the feeling that something, or someone, is trying to catch your attention, like an odd voice speaking to you from some other place.

In your mind, you run to it because you want to hear more of the voice. You want to see more of the flickering. You lose yourself in the transcendence of the moment, and wonder where it all comes from. When you get to the café, you tell your friends about the intense sunrise that spoke to you. Everyone sips and smiles and continues on. Though you cannot explain it, the sunrise encounter feels tangible.

There is something more out there. You just can't put your finger on it. The language beaming from the light and the oak tree limbs feels like a language you were born to understand. You know in your heart that the sense of wonder found in the idea of a sunrise, unlike everything else that will fade and die, will always remain. It is eternal.

———

In contrast to the language of culture, another language exists. The transcendent language symbolized by the fall sunrise.[2] This language points us to our true existence— toward honesty and meaning and deep relationships. It sees the "hollow man" pursuit of the world and instead pushes toward a renewal of the inner self. It is the language of God.

When we hear the language of God in *relationships*, in *love*, and in *an abiding life*, our shallow life of worldly desires is replaced with a full life, focused on others. We find that our relationships develop into something deeper than casual conversations and surface-level understandings of each other. They move past the computer screen and into the tangible day-to-day. Instead of worrying about impressing our friends and loved ones, we are strengthened to be honest and to develop our relationships in a deep way.

We see a love built upon something that the world

doesn't have time or room for: sacrifice. The language of culture rejects the idea of putting yourself last, whereas the language of God celebrates others and works toward making them better.

In the language of God, we find the Way toward a life that abides in the comforts of our Creator, one that recognizes our true selves through our ultimate relationship with him.

The veneer produced by the language of culture keeps us, ultimately, from the deep relational language of God. At our core, we hunger for deep relationships. Theologian Alistair McFadyen says that Christ calls us into the dialogue of relationships, and that as we participate in these dialogues, we change and even rise above the self-serving nature of the world's fractured structures.[3] "Christ is beyond us," writes McFadyen. "From this transcendent position he comes to us, calls us to Him and so calls us to become what we truly are." This, then, is the prize for all humanity – to find our true selves resting in Christ and then reflected in our relationships with others.

God created us to be relational. Our relationship with him acts as a center for all our earthly ones, "pulling us towards God and others."[4] But if that relationship suffers from estrangement, then our interactions with one another will feel the lack.

True, we are fallen and broken people, but in our relationship with God through Christ, we do have hope. "We are afflicted in every way, but not crushed; perplexed, but not despairing; persecuted, but not forsaken; struck down, but not destroyed; always carrying about in the body the dying of Jesus, so that the life of Jesus also may be manifested in our body."

God made a way for all of humankind to come to him.

"Therefore we do not lose heart, but though our outer man is decaying, yet our inner man is being renewed day by day. For momentary, light affliction is producing for us an eternal weight of glory far beyond all comparison, while we look not at the things which are seen, but at the things which are not seen; for the things which are seen are temporal, but the things which are not seen are eternal."[5]

Chapter Six

WHALE STARS

Encountering the Magnificent

BEHOLD, THE DWELLING PLACE
OF GOD IS WITH MAN.

— Revelation 21:3 ESV

If you ever have the chance, do yourself a favor and explore the Four Corners area where New Mexico, Colorado, Utah, and Arizona all meet. It's the kind of place that feels like God took extra care to create. In New Mexico, you can drive a hundred miles in any direction, stop the car, and step out into the resounding silence of a mesa desert where the silence hovers, permeating the entire region.

The Durango silence differs; there, Colorado's San Juan Mountains rifle up toward the sky, thick with bristle cone pine and aspens. Creeks and rivers knife down and through the mountains, splashing liquid white upon the outdoor canvas. And then there's the sound. At 4:00 a.m. on a clear June night, you can see just enough of your surroundings to feel uneasy. All is still, except for the air whistling ever so gently through the pines while the aspen leaves rustle their approval. And when you look up, through the trees, the stars jump out of the darkness like millions of surfacing whales, majestic and fearsome.

Beneath the canopy, you can barely see your campsite. If not for the whale stars, all would be black. As you stand outside your tent, you can hear your heart beating, but just barely. The silence has a rhythm—the cadence of the leaves, the flow of the rushing water, and the crackle of a neighboring fire. These are the sounds of the San Juan silence, and they are wonderfully deafening.

Next, head west, just over the mountains, to Moab, Utah. Grab some java at Mondo Coffee and hit the Porcupine Rim trail on your mountain bike or take a jeep tour of the red desert. Then, continue northwest and spend the night in Bryce Canyon.

In Bryce, another kind of silence awaits, the brilliant kind. Camp near the rim of the canyon if you can. There are plenty of sites. Do your best to wake up well before the dawn. Hike over to Sunrise Point and set up your camp chair facing east over the canyon. And wait. If you have coffee, bring it; you may also want your journal.

From this vantage point, you will be able to see more stars than you ever thought possible. They are not the same whale stars from Durango; these are the minions of God—the infinite army of light soldiers, their shields shimmering like a pirate's treasure. They're a spectacle so vivid you can decipher them by color and size. But this is not why you're sitting here.

As the sun gets closer to the horizon, the stars fade and the canyon begins to wake. All the hoodoo rock formations with their red-rock hues come into view, and you begin to see the valley stretch out before you. The thin mountain air crystallizes the view. And then it happens: the first peek of sunlight emerges, shouting past the horizon like a growling giant. The canyon explodes with color. The sky bleeds into a rainbow while the canyon dances in shadows and light.

The sound is brilliant, painted with color and majesty and wonder, and a touch of magic. As you watch it all unfold, you gasp. Again, you can hear your heart beating, fast. You breathe in while your eyes dart from canyon to sun to sky to journal. Nothing more to do but sit and listen and watch.

The weight of silence, the fullness of solitude—we are not familiar with either. They seem strange and uncomfortable to us. And yet within them are the deep murmurings of God.

You will, undoubtedly, be hard pressed to find a place devoid of sound, so perhaps the better idea of silence rests in the act of being quiet, hushing your words to hear God's. And doing so in a place of beauty, removed from distractions.

The Four Corners' version of silence and solitude is grand. Its massiveness makes you feel insignificant. If you've ever rappelled down a sheer Sierra Nevada cliff or dropped two hundred feet into the pitch black belly of a mountain, then you know the feeling of complete help-lessness – your heart beating in your ears, your mind racing through death scenarios. Fear and exhilaration fill the encounter. The allure of this part of the country rests in its wildness and unpredictability. At any moment, you could be crushed by its immensity. It drips with holy grandeur, like God is hovering over and breathing down on the land.

Who is God to you?

When you daily approach him, how do you do it? What motivates you? Do you come to him with a scripted mindset as if you were taking a vacation to Disney World where you know exactly what to expect? Do you bank on God's being and acting a certain way?

Or do you approach him with zero expectations?[1] The same way you'd approach hiking a newfound trail. You would start walking, taking in the view. Nothing scripted, nothing predictable.

What do you bring before him? Do you bring him the cracked vessel of *you*? Or do you bring him a veneered you, the lost and afraid you?

What does it mean to worship him?

As we reflect on the Four Corners' landscape, there is

much we learn about God. We find that when confronted with silence and openness and majesty and wonder and solitude, we are deeply moved, so touched by it that we don't speak; it feels silly to do so. We don't move. We watch the sun over Bryce Canyon and are left breathless. We stare at the whale stars and listen to the mountain creeks in Durango and feel like we need to remain still.

God is like this, though we don't take the time to see him as such. Too often we treat him as our pocket Savior, our own personal Jesus, or our political fail-safe or maybe even our get-out-of-jail-free card for a way of living we know isn't on the up and up.

"If you have only come the length of asking God for things," writes minister and teacher Oswald Chambers, "you have never come to the first strand of abandonment, you have become a Christian from a standpoint of your own."[2] And this will not fly. We cannot approach God as though he were a cosmic superstore. We must be willing to hold the relational position of self-abandonment.

But this kind of language seems strange to us. Self-abandonment? Isn't this the society in which the pursuit of self gets rewarded? Do we not promote language like "positive self-speak" and "leveraging influence" and "expressing yourself"? In our society, if you're not leveraging or maximizing something, you're underachieving.

The apostle Paul had it right when he wrote to his apprentice Timothy and said, "In the last days ... people will be lovers of self, lovers of money, proud, arrogant, abusive ... unholy."[3] But our society didn't arrive at this place where we so unabashedly celebrate self quickly. It was a slow burn from virtue, a universal measuring stick for right personal behavior, to values, a personal preference meter showing what behaviors are important to an individual.

Historian Gertrude Himmelfarb points to philosopher Friedrich Nietzsche as one of the forerunners of the self movement. Nietzsche wanted to get rid of a standard of morality (especially as it related to Christianity) and reduce it to a subjective take on behavior. If he had his way, everyone would be able to decide what was right in their own eyes, their own set of values. As it turns out, Nietzsche's world of power and self-reliance stares each of us in the face every day.

Modern society gravitated to Nietzsche's ideas because they fit nicely in the enlightened structure of look what we can know; look what we can do. "Values brought with it the assumptions that all moral ideas are subjective and relative," writes Himmelfarb, "that they are mere customs and conventions, that they are purely instrumental, utilitarian purposes, and that they are peculiar to specific individuals and societies."[4]

For more than a century, much of the advanced world has been on a collision course with total autonomy – man, apart from God. Today, Nietzsche's self-movement takes on multiple forms. From self-help, to self-realization, to health-and-wealth, we are neck deep in the self.

Theologian John Stott, in *The Cross of Christ*, reminds us how the Christian subculture has bought into this mindset, using Jesus' "great commandment" as justification to love the self. When asked which is the great commandment in the law, Jesus replied, "You shall love the Lord your God with all your heart and with all your soul and with all your mind. This is the great and first commandment. And a second is like it: You shall love your neighbor as yourself."[5]

The hierarchy of Jesus' words cannot be overlooked here. He answers with the familiar words of the *shema* – heart, soul, mind – taken from the Old Testament law and interestingly replaces "might" with "mind," which no doubt made the message relatable in a Greek culture that prized philosophy. The second command, Jesus says, is *like* the first, and so we can understand that it might be an action that flows from loving God. The second commandment ends with "as yourself," which is not a command but the understood starting point for loving others.

"Self-love," writes Stott, "is a fact to be recognized and rule to be used, not a virtue to be commended."[6] In Christ's redeeming act—his death on the Roman cross—we have the encouragement to find ourselves again, through the new life that his death brings. So yes, Christ affirms us in that though we were dead in our sins, we are now new creatures.[7] But this new life models itself after Christ—a narrow pathway.

Paul warns us in Romans to view ourselves with "sober judgment,"[8] carrying the confidence of the cross but with a spirit of service and self-abandonment. No matter how much we try to skew the Christian life, we cannot wiggle away from Christ's own challenge to his disciples: "If anyone would come after me, let him deny himself and take up his cross and follow me."[9]

Christ's love rises in the form of his cross, marking the Christian faith with sacrificial love. "The cross of Christ supplies the answer, for it calls us both to self-denial and to self-affirmation."[10] So through Christ, we find that grace transforms us out of our fallenness and that mercy challenges us to follow after Christ himself, a way of life wholly other.

Life's realities make following along this narrow path difficult. It can be lonely. We'd rather be friends with God and fall into a nonchalant faith of church attendance and worship events than to seek him in the brilliant silence. Many of us are frustrated in our spiritual lives because we feel like God doesn't hear us. But should that frustration surprise us when we ask of him from a position of selfishness?

As Chambers challenges, we have to ask ourselves, What aren't we willing to give up? What will we *not* do?[11]

And so, we continue to exist on the other side of self-abandonment, the side of self-love. Seventy-five years ago, poet T. S. Eliot wrote,

> O world of spring and autumn, birth and dying!
> The endless cycle of idea and action,
> Endless invention, endless experiment,
> Brings knowledge of motion, but not of stillness;
> Knowledge of speech, but not of silence;
> Knowledge of words, and ignorance of the Word.
> All our knowledge brings us nearer to death,
> But nearness to death no nearer to God.
> Where is the Life we have lost in living?
> Where is the wisdom we have lost in knowledge?
> Where is the knowledge we have lost in information?
> The cycles of Heaven in twenty centuries
> Brings us farther from God and nearer to the Dust.[12]

Eliot's words are familiar to us. Not because we have read them before but because we have lived them and are living them. In gaining the world, we refuse to abandon the self. We are nearer to the dust and have nothing to show for it.

———

To encounter the grandeur of the Four Corners, you have to go there. And when you do, the heavy silence and vast solitude are waiting, by-products of the journey to this splendid destination. God should be a daily destination for us. He should be one with whom we seek audience, a place we long to be in, a river we seek to wash in, a canyon we want to get lost in.

We need to go *to* God and then stop. We need to lay down our burdens and requests for a moment and attempt to gather him in, encountering his vastness. We do not approach him with a laundry list of wants. Rather, we approach him in order to worship him—giving him his worth—hoping that by being in his presence, we will glean a small piece of his glory to season our daily existence.

But our society makes it difficult for us to fully understand what it means to encounter God in this way. Thanks to philosophers like Nietzsche, personal experience in our society trumps even propositional truth, and we use experience as our doping needle for the transcendent. We think that if we can manipulate experiences, the world will feel better. We will *be* better.

Our society drips with manufactured experiences. Getting coffee has to be a heightened sensory experience, not a dry retail transaction. Some of us bristle over the fact that we must make everything an experience in order for it to feel better than it really is. And in some ways, we are right to think this way, for it exposes us as fiercely relational creatures. We so desperately long to experience the transcendent that we design the inanimate world — computers, coffee, shopping — to make it feel dynamic.

In life, we pass from one experience to the other. And each experience lasts only a few moments until a better more memorable one replaces it. We pile our experiences high, and though they shape us to some extent, they do not understand or know us. When was the last time you told someone, "Yeah, I hung out with Jonathan today. *He* was a great experience"? You might say, "Jonathan and I went to the waterfall today; what a cool experience." We speak of experiences in the past tense, and though they often include people, experiences aren't people. Experiences are great, but by definition, they are merely emotional, self-focused events.[13]

At the end of the day, our experiences turn to mere memories. We feel like something's changed about us. But experiences, though they are part of life, leave us just as alone as we were before. If we focus only on experience, we miss the most important part of the life equation: encounter.

―――

Think about the whale stars. Think about peeking through the ponderosa pine and seeing a few falling stars light up the sky. After it happens, you feel like you have to tell someone; you feel like you just stole something so beautiful from the sky and you can't even explain why. You're dizzy with excitement.

That's how our interaction with God should be. When we seek encounters with God, we never know what to expect. He's as unpredictable as a fall day in the Colorado Rockies. Why can't our worship gatherings reflect this truth about God? Maybe because most of us like to plan for God like we plan for the weather.

Theologian Eugene Peterson has written on the idea of modern-day worship. In a section of *The Jesus Way* where he discusses Elijah's confrontation with the Baal worshipers, Peterson talks about the harlotry metaphor used in the Old Testament to refer to the literal prostitution of the Baal cult. But then he extends the metaphor and uses it to form a theology of worship. He writes, " 'Harlotry' is worship that says, 'I will give you satisfaction. You want religious feelings? I will give them to you.... I'll do it in the form most arousing to you' ... Baalism reduces worship to the spiritual stature of the worshiper. Its canons are that it should be interesting, relevant, and exciting – that I 'get something out of it.'"[14]

When we make worship a sensory experience, we devalue its authenticity. The primary focus, which should be on God, turns to those manipulating the experience.

What if we actually took a break from the everyday so we could encounter God as he is? God doesn't speak to us through the cool of culture; he speaks in gentle whispers. Augustine says that God does not speak with man through the medium of matter but "by means of the truth itself." What would happen to us as the church if we walked in on Sunday completely open and broken before God, ready to encounter his ravishing Spirit and Word?

Unlike *experience*, the word *encounter* carries a relational meaning. It can mean "a chance meeting" or "a hostile confrontation." So let's ask ourselves: is God more an event that we attend to accumulate knowledge or is he a being whom we meet with or even clash with? Does he reveal himself throughout the world in creation and through his Word? Do we not have very deep ways to come up against his vast and untamed glory?

There is a highway in the Four Corners area called the Million Dollar Highway. It will scare you to death, because "highway" is a misnomer. It's really just a two-lane twelve-mile pass with no guardrails south of Uncompahgre Gorge in southern Colorado. On it, you're exposed to high winds. It's like driving on a tightrope with steep cliffs on both sides. You doze off on this road, you're a goner.

This "highway" represents the unexpected, the untamed insanity you find all over the Four Corners. You cannot sidestep the highway; you must drive it. You must expose yourself to the elements and the danger to feel the rush of excitement before you get to the other end of the pass and a road that feels more familiar. You must come up against this road and its startling makeup. It is only in descending the pass that you can talk about the experience, how you were surprised and afraid.

When we attend worship services that allow us to stop in and see God, who is he *really* to us? Is he not more than this?

Who is God if not the divine Father whom we encounter with awe and reverence, fire devouring before him and around him a tempest raging?[15] Who is God if not the Son, the head of the church, whom we encounter together, corporately, speaking truth and love to one another, growing into him who is our Head?[16] Who is God if not the Holy Spirit, whom we encounter within—our Great Teacher, Counselor, and Reminder of Truth?[17] God did not create humankind to *experience* us and then walk away. He created humankind to walk with us, to love us, and for us to be loved by him.

Experiences and encounters differ. One smacks of selfish gratification: we love to experience because we love to feel. The other intimates relation. Paul the apostle did not have a mere supernatural experience on the road to Damascus. He encountered the resurrected Christ. This encounter changed the entire trajectory of Paul's life, because he was confronted with the *person* of Jesus.

When we exchange a true encounter with God for a veneered experience that satisfies our selfish desires, we proclaim the self above God.

———

When we talk about encounter, we must address the relational element. Think about life as if it were one giant conversation. Self-abandonment demands that we live as people taking part in the conversation. Conversation is a dialogue between two or more people, which makes those we live with and among part of the dialogue. There is give and take, reciprocity, and confrontation. We serve the conversation when we listen, considering the other person's needs more important than our own. It can be a beautiful dance.

But when we live experientially, the dialogue breaks down; it becomes one-sided, a monologue. In a monologue, only one person speaks, only one person matters. A monologuer does not stand in a position of true relationship. He stands alone, barking lines to everyone.

It's the same in life. If we live like the monologuer, we begin to use people as leverage devices, seen only for their use to our particular needs. Our interactions with them turn into a power, dominance, and manipulation structure and less of a relationship. The monologuer does not need interaction, because he just wants to control people and events. To the monologuer, people exist as a means to success. He does not understand others, nor is he understood. He speaks, and lives, to hear his own voice.[18]

Chances are that if we treat other people this way, we treat God this way too. We fail to realize that he originated the dialogue and that he longs to interact with us. Prayer is our means to speak and interact with him. Theologian Peter Jensen says that prayer's "scope, content, and assurance are based on the character of God as he reveals himself." The fact that we can have real interaction with the God of the universe is staggering. It's a reality that comes to life when you walk outside during a fall sunset, see the colors, and whisper to God. Eyes filling up and heart bursting, you hear his voice. You shudder.

The monologuer, in his line barking, sees the world as his audience, the stage meant only for him. He speaks from a position "of his own," as Chambers puts it. Stiff and rigid, brash and bold, the monologuer loses out on the expected beauty and romance of dialogue with God. For there must be tender compliance as we speak to and with God. As the Teacher reminds us in Ecclesiastes, we must come first to listen, keeping our words few and our hearts open, ready for the radiance of the Father.[19]

In his book *Prayer*, Richard Foster talks about how approaching God while "completely abandoned to the hands of God"[20] can deepen us. Again we run into the idea of self-abandonment. Our greatest act toward God is a life offering, one ready for his will alone.

To Foster, prayer — dialogue with God — sweetens our relationship with God and sets our course in life toward the consummation of that relationship. But as well-seasoned monologuers, we must drop the act and everything that goes with it. We must allow ourselves to be stripped down so we are unencumbered by our barking lines.

———

The Four Corners area feels like a frontier we can all learn from — just wild enough to scare us a bit but tame enough to invite us in. If we are daring, we can experience it to the fullest. If we are patient, though, the experience will blossom into something grand because of our encounter.

If you visit, amid the Bryce Canyon sunrise or the rushing Durango mountain sounds, you will come face to face with God. And the greatest part of being out there is that you cannot turn to leave when you start to feel uncomfortable. The grandeur and silence have a way of pressing down into your soul. If you abide there long enough, you will find all your secret thoughts exposed, waving in the mountain air. No place for veneer. Just you and God, if you dare encounter him, if you dare enter into conversation with him.

In the same way, we need a new spiritual home, a spiritual frontier. A place where the light of love is somehow changed and odd, like at Bryce Canyon. A place like the desert mesas of New Mexico that will serve as the hovering spot for God. A place where wonder echoes throughout the landscape of our souls.

This spiritual frontier, this holy *other* place, is within a breath of praise and a whisper of humility. But the world drowns out the magnificent and overwhelms us with the mediocre. Veneer overruns us so much that we don't even care to encounter God. Maybe on Tuesdays and Thursdays after yoga, but even then it's a tight squeeze. We have, in our haste, pushed God to the margins.

We must fight to regain God as our center. A prayer, a cry, whatever it takes to find him once again as the frontier of our very being. Living from a divine center can happen only if we understand what it means to live before God, all the time. Being centered on God takes time and effort. It takes a conscious mind to engage in the divine conversation.

A. W. Tozer, in his book *The Pursuit of God*, writes, "There must be somewhere a fixed center against which everything else is measured, where the law of relativity does not enter and we can say 'IS' and make no allowances. Such a center is God."[21] As we focus on who God is and what it means to live before him, we find in him much that overwhelms.

"We feel honestly the pull of many obligations and try to fulfill them all," writes Thomas Kelley. "And we are unhappy, uneasy, strained, oppressed, and fearful we shall be hollow ... We have hints that there is a way of life vastly richer and deeper than all this hurried existence, a life of unhurried serenity and peace and power. If only we could slip over into that Center."[22]

Alistair McFadyen, Richard Foster, A. W. Tozer, and Thomas Kelley all remind us how important it is to live life from the divine center. The concept demands our reflection and our emulation. It's no secret formula and doesn't instantly make us spiritual gurus. It is, rather, a call to brothers and sisters, a call to come out in the wilderness of God and be surprised by him once again.

———

When our selfish desires motivate us to approach God with a laundry list, we find that our faith fails to shimmer. Perhaps we approach God in this way because we do not see him properly. Think for a moment. How do you view God? Who is he to you? When you close your eyes and reflect on his being—his majesty, grandeur, and wonder—what images blaze through your brain?

When we first come to God, young in the faith, our thoughts of him tend to exist in the area of "God as our salvation" or "God as life preserver." Sadly, many of us never get past this phase of our relationship with him.

But for those who dare to pursue God, who wander under the whale stars and seek his face, his great and unfathomable mystery will slowly unfold. In this pursuit, we find we must slow down from the everyday and listen to him and wait on him. When we do this, our perspective changes. We begin to think God's thoughts after him. The closer we get to him, the deeper we slip away from the self that so often blinds us. We see God crystallize over our lifetime, and suddenly the world fades from the foreground to the background.

———

God is the great unknown, and this confuses us. The same reason we fear stepping off the edge to rappel down the cliff is the same reason we don't often like to be alone in our thoughts with God. Our minds, inevitably, swim out into an open space like the ocean or the never-ending horizon or some other uncharted vastness. Uneasiness settles in, like when we dove in to the deep end of the pool for the first time. We end up frightened, swimming back to the shores of our more comfortable thoughts.

But what if he were to meet us on those safe and familiar shores? What if God came to us? What would he be doing? What would he say? What would you say?

Chapter Seven

THE VIOLENCE OF BEES

Discovering a True Relationship

THERE'S A LOT OF THINGS I DON'T UNDERSTAND,

WHY SO MANY PEOPLE LIE.

IT'S THE HURT I HIDE THAT FUELS THE FIRE INSIDE ME.

WILL I ALWAYS FEEL THIS WAY?

SO EMPTY, SO ESTRANGED.

– Ray LaMontagne, "Empty"

Imagine you're walking on the safe shores of life. You visit these shores often because you can see the untamed ocean from a distance while sitting in relative comfort and safety. Rumors suggest that God is somewhere far out there, and though this intrigues you, you've figured out a way to keep his Son, Jesus, somewhere close by on the safe shores.

It's been a while, however, since you visited Jesus; you've been busy with your career, and, well, you're just busy. Today, though, you thought you'd walk the coastline and maybe even rent a boat and row out a ways, see what you find. And maybe you'd happen upon some luck and run into Jesus along the way.

It's a rocky coast, like Maine's, and down the coastline you see what looks like smoke. You get closer and notice a man stooping beside a fire. It smells inviting, so you approach him, not realizing at first that it *is* Jesus.

You're still a few yards off, but you offer a "how's it going?" as he cooks fish over the open fire. He's looking out into the distance, just smiling.

You're close enough and can feel the fire now. And as

you stop to greet him, the horizon catches your eye. Its incandescent light casts itself all over the breaking waves. He sits poking the fire and humming, his weathered skin buffeted by the salty air. He looks up at you as you gaze out into the distance. You turn your head toward the fire to catch him looking at you; he seems familiar, but you still don't recognize him. He nods and smiles.

"Are you heading out there?"

"I was thinking about it. Not sure though," you reply.

"I wouldn't go too far out if I were you. It's not safe."

"Why? I've heard that God's out there somewhere. I wonder if he would notice me."

"*I* notice you."

The words come to you like spring, like blowing on a child's face; there is loss of breath and exhilaration all at once.

"But who are *you?*"

"I AM the horizon. I AM the rain. I AM the good. I AM the radiance you feel when you get too far out there. I AM victory; sometimes you feel me, though not as often as you should. I AM the light you saw in your grandmother before she passed. I AM the joy you felt when your daughter was born. I AM glory. I AM the breath of creation. I AM."

He looks up from the cooking fish, his eyes filling up,

but you turn your head away, again looking out into the horizon. And then it dawns on you.

Why didn't I recognize him? you ask yourself.

He looks back down and flips the fish. The gray of the evening shrouds him.

"I'm sorry, I ..." your words feel heavy, "I had no idea."

"I know," he replies. "I'm not who you remember me to be. I've passed you on this coastline before, but you didn't notice. You looked stressed and busy." He half laughs and wipes his tearing eyes. "I think you like the idea of me. But you'd rather I remain out of the way."

His words cut at your insides. But he's right.

"I remember when you used to seek me out all the time," he continues. "I loved our relationship. But something changed. What happened?"

"I don't know."

———

Apologist Ravi Zacharias says that in the Christian faith, love precedes life.[1] Using this cosmic time line, we can trace our existence all the way back to love. When we time-travel back to the early days before God created Adam and Eve, when "God's Spirit brooded like a bird above the watery abyss," we find our origin. We tend to think in terms of being created by God, which is true. But we often forget that God is not a mono God; he is the Three-in-One God. We were created out of a loving community known as the Holy Trinity. So when Dr. Zacharias says that love precedes life, he is pointing us to God in community with the Son and the Spirit.[2]

We are born with a proclivity to love and to be loved. We are born for relationship, fashioned after a prototype: the Holy Trinity. We exist *as* people and we pattern our lives *around* other people. We live in relation to our parents and friends and God and the world around us. We understand this idea of relation because we feel the repercussions of our relationships on a daily basis.

Some of us live in the pain of isolation. Others live in the angst of bitterness. Still others barely exist, scraping along life's sewer in despair, alone and wishing for someone to reach out a hand. Life abounds with the watermarks of relationships. We love, we hate, we cheat, we lie, we praise, we encourage, all out of the need and unabated drive to relate to others.

Philosopher Cornelius Plantinga calls the very act of creation "an act of imaginative love." Not only does God, in his vast and unsearchable mind, create humankind but he does so out of joy. He does so to love, for he is the first lover. Plantinga writes, "God cannot be God without relationships, but it doesn't follow that God needs a world in order to have them ... [He] overflows with regard for others ... It was so much *like* God to create, to imagine possible worlds and then to actualize one of them."[3]

Plantinga is referring to the relationship between God the Father and the Son and the Spirit, who share in a love that existed before time. Humankind, therefore, can claim an existence based on a preexisting heavenly love. This fact helps us understand that we receive our hunger for relationships from this diverse and holy unity. And when we begin to view ourselves through the kaleidoscope of the Holy Trinity, we begin to view our earthly relationships differently.

Understanding the relational quality of the Trinity helps us formulate important questions about our makeup and purpose in this world. What is the difference, for example, between being created out of necessity and being created from love? Maybe we answer with another question: who wants to exist because we have to? Where is the love or eternal possibility in that? Think about a one-dimensional god who exists unto himself, not in relation. That god *has to create* in order to love. If we were simply created from necessity, then we exist because we have to. What a devaluing notion.

But if we were created out of love, to be in relationship with God the Father, his unique Son, and the Holy Spirit, then we find ourselves drenched in the colors of their kaleidoscopic love, moving and swirling in a divine relationship. There was a purpose and intent in God's creative act, like a focused artist crafting his masterpiece. Maybe this is why the apostle Paul calls us God's *poiema*, his workmanship. And this notion comforts us. We can almost see that when God breathed the breath of life into man, he also breathed love, and when he fashioned woman out of a man's rib, he built her with care and lovingkindness.

But why would the triune God want to create humankind in the first place? Maybe one day the idea came upon the Father, and the Son and the Spirit agreed that it was a good idea. We don't know. But consider the incredible solace in knowing that out of such a tremendous love, God created. "I cannot help it," says the Father to the Son. "I simply must create. To love is to *be*." All the while, the Spirit dances in joy over the creation.

And now, here we are on the other side of eternity, struggling to find our place in a world we don't understand, struggling to find one another in the dark, struggling to find someone who will love us.

But too often we back away from God because he confronts us too deeply, forcing us into a place of uncertainty. And uncertainty scares us. We like knowing what's going to happen next; we enjoy being in control. We don't like the feeling we get when we stand under the whale stars for too long, God's whispers invading our hearts. We'd rather sit among our glorious stuff, keeping God at arm's length.

So we do our best to constrain God to our limited space and time, giving him cues for when he can appear in life, always making sure he's in his box. In our attempt to limit his influence on our lives, we forget that he's relational. We forget him as Father and Son and Spirit. Instead, we think about him as a cosmic do-gooder or an entity either disconnected from the human condition of war, disease, and unrest, or worse, unwilling to end it.

If only we could daily see God in light of his totality, his trinity. What a beautiful thing. It's easy to think that Jesus exists outside of current life and context and only in our Sunday routine. But we do this to our detriment. For he is our advocate when despondency takes hold. He wants us to lean into the massive community of his being. But we like to keep him in our two-thousand-year-old stories.

What then? Is the Trinity so removed from our daily lives that we cling to that which we can see, touch, and hold? Consider God as your father, maybe the father you never had. How does God in this role affect your life? How might you begin to interact with him if you viewed him as your Abba, Father?

Think of Jesus, the Son—God among us. In the Gospels, we see him traveling with his disciples, healing lepers, helping prostitutes, touching blind eyes, telling riddles, celebrating at a wedding feast, weeping for a friend, violently protecting the sacred, praying alone on a mountainside, speaking to the wind and calming the storm, cooking fish for Peter and the disciples on the beach, face to face with Satan, baptized by his second cousin, eating and drinking with the corrupt and wicked, challenging his friends to follow him to death, abandoned by those closest to him, beaten, spit on, condemned, and silent. Is he not someone in whom we can relate? Is he not someone in whom we can trust? Was killing him not enough for us to see his humanity? Was his resurrection not enough to strike our hearts with awe and thanksgiving? He is the God-man.

And he left for us the blessing of the Holy Spirit.

"I will talk to the Father, and he'll provide you another Friend so that you will always have someone with you. This Friend is the Spirit of Truth. The godless world can't take him in because it doesn't have eyes to see him, doesn't know what to look for. But you know him already because he has been staying with you, and will even be in you!"[4]

We cannot see the Spirit, only the effects of the Spirit. Yet there are even those in the church who claim they cannot sense the Spirit in their lives. But he lives inside us. He convicts us, and the world; he listens to the moans and groans of our hearts. He is now our great advocate.

Perhaps it's not that we don't sense him but that we ignore his voice. He reaches for our hand, but we pull away. "The Spirit of the Truth, he will take you by the hand and guide you into all the truth there is."[5]

Our relationship with the Spirit works the same as any other relationship. We should take great care to listen to him. To be still, and listen.

———

Back on the rocky shore, your discussion with Jesus continues. After handing you a plate of food and gathering up more wood for the fire, he invites you to stay longer and talk. You oblige and begin eating, but the conversation takes a turn.

"Thanks for being patient with me in all of this."

"Sure," he replies.

"Hearing you talk about the relationship you have with your Father and the Spirit reminds me of my family. I'm not doing very well on that front lately. I think sometimes I just get so into myself that I fail to see how my relationships shape me."

"It's easy to do in this world; things have become so crazy," he replies.

Resting your plate on the sand, you lean back on one of the driftwood logs and survey the horizon.

"What's really out there?" you ask. "Why did you caution me about wandering too far out?"

"Well, you could die. Even here on the shore, you are at risk."

"I don't want to die. I guess I just want to know who God is. But I don't like the thought of going all the way out there. It makes me feel sick, like my heart is about to collapse."

He nods. "It's part of who you are to want that. But you were separated long ago."

His comment startles you. You don't remember that part of the story. It seems unfair.

"But you don't have to go out there," he continues. "Just talk to me."

"So if I can't go out there, how will I ever get to him?"

"*I* will get you to him. That's what he sent me here to do."

———

Fierce. It means "having or displaying an intense or ferocious aggressiveness; showing a heartfelt intensity; powerful and destructive in extent."[6] We tend to think of this word in relation to professional athletes or soldiers. It carries the idea of a person striving after something with unbridled passion, not letting go until they win the prize.

But what would it mean for God to be fierce? How would that change our view of him? How would knowing a fierce God change *us*?

Think on this statement: "God loves us something fierce."[7] If you heard someone say that to you, how would you explain it? If God loves us with an aggressiveness and heartfelt intensity, then he would be a God who not only receives love from us, his creation, but also seeks and pursues us.

Like the father running to his prodigal son, who was lost to him, God runs after us and embraces us as his own. When we think of God's love as fierce, we can immediately see it in the crucifixion of Christ. "This is how much God loved the world," writes John the Beloved, "He gave his Son."[8] He didn't have to come after us the way he did. He didn't have to "make a way," knowing that only the death of his unique Son was that way. He didn't have to, but he did.

It's just like Jesus' words back on the beach: "*I* will get you to him." And he did so through an obedient love. He did so through a self-abandoned pursuit – of you.

This holy pursuit by God makes it possible for us to come to him now, through Jesus. "You wiped out all the evils which merited punishment," writes Augustine in his *Confessions*, "so as not to bring the due reward upon my hands, by which I fell away from you ... Before I existed you were, and I had no being to which you could grant existence. Nevertheless here I am as a result of your goodness, which goes before all that you made me to be and all out of which you made me."[9]

Like Augustine, here we are, a result of God's goodness and his endless pursuit, able to come into beautiful relationship with him. In his letter to Titus, Paul writes, "He *saved* us not by works of righteousness that we have done but on the basis of his mercy, through the washing of the new birth and the renewing of the Holy Spirit."[10] There was no virtue we could offer, no moral good that he would accept. And yet he reached out to us and rescued us from "the pit of oblivion."[11]

"You had no need of me," continues Augustine. "I do not possess such goodness as to give you help, my Lord and my God."[12] God turns our wretchedness into righteousness, offering us the Way, the Truth, and the Life, with him, and through him.

But we don't always understand the dynamic that comes from having a relationship with Jesus in this way. Too often we view our position before God as lowly wretch or worm. We forget that God not only extends eternal life to us but also adopts us into his eternal family. He transforms us from paupers to princes, fellow heirs of his glory. The garden of Eden wasn't a cosmic experiment for God to discover what would happen to humankind on planet Earth. It was the beginning point for God's creating his extended family.[13]

Why is it so important that we not overlook God's fierce love for humankind? Because it's in that fierceness that we realize that we are born from God.[14] It's in that fierceness that we find the heavenly Father rescuing his children from the blackest darkness of a world enslaved to sin. And it's in this rescue story that we find one of the most beautiful ideas of God: adoption.

In Galatians, Paul writes, "God sent him to buy freedom for us who were slaves to the law, so that he could adopt us as his very own children."[15] For those who haven't adopted, this language loses some of its impact. But for others, who have been through the adoption process, Paul's allusion makes perfect sense.

Imagine one day you open the mailbox and discover the package you had anticipated for some time: a large yellow packet addressed to you from the state. Excited, you dart into the house and slice open the envelope. You already know the contents; inside awaits the formality of a year's worth of chasing the unknown. Pursuing a strange love that you can never fully explain.

Inside, the proof of existence – a birth certificate. The daughter you never expected, adopted into your family. You had nothing to do with her conception, nor were you present when she entered the world, yet your name appears on the document as her father. Your wife, listed as her mother. Your family name, given to her.

Weeks earlier, you stood before a judge as he made legal something that was set in motion before time began. A mere formality at that point, he declared the child legally yours. The cold and lifeless back room of the courthouse transformed itself from a place of strict legal proceedings to one of mysterious love.

People often stop you in the store and ask, "Are you her dad?" You hate that question; of course she is yours. God gave her to you. But you and your daughter look nothing alike, you don't even have the same color skin. Even so, sometimes at night when dressing her for bed, you look at her and think, *She has my eyes.*

You will help her learn to read and to tie her shoes and to ride a bike. You will sit shotgun as she takes her first driving lesson. You will snap one hundred pictures as she walks down the stairs in her graduation gown. And one day in the not too distant future, you will hold her hand as she walks down the wedding aisle. "Who gives this woman to be married to this man?" "Her mother and I do," you'll answer. You will cry.

In this view of adoption, we catch a small glimpse of the immense and eternal love of God, our Father. He adopted us. He waited in the back of a courthouse to make us his son. His daughter. In this life, we will never fully grasp the gravity of our spiritual adoption. But we know it is as real. As real as the yellow packet.

Adoption gives us the ability to answer God's call. We are his sheep, and we answer because we *do* know our names: we are his children. "So you have not received a spirit that makes you fearful slaves. Instead, you received God's Spirit when he adopted you as his own children. Now we call him, 'Abba, Father.' ... And we believers also groan, even though we have the Holy Spirit within us as a foretaste of future glory, for we long for our bodies to be released from sin and suffering. We, too, wait with eager hope for the day when God will give us our full rights as his adopted children."[16]

Spiritual adoption carries the expectations of the Father. J. I. Packer says that there are three all-encompassing principles related to Christian conduct. First, we are to imitate our Father, which is not hard for us to understand. Many of us wanted to be like our moms or dads or crazy uncles. We imitated them whenever we could. Our heavenly Father asks us to "be holy, as I am holy." He tells us, his children, to run after him, to imitate him not just in his moral goodness but in his set-apartness. The idea of children imitating their father was a familiar one to the Jews. Several times in the Old Testament book of Leviticus, God tells Israel to be holy, to consecrate themselves to him, to imitate him. If we are to imitate God in his purity and righteousness, then what place does the language of culture have in our lives, especially if it draws away from intimacy with our heavenly Father? We are his kids now, so we should act like it.

Next, Packer says we should glorify the Father. "Christians," he writes, "must seek to behave in public in a way that brings praise to their Father in heaven."[17] In a veneered world, this can be challenging. It is easy to act in a way that elevates personal agendas or status. But if we purpose in our minds that everything we do and say brings glory to our Father, then the world will take notice.

Growing up, we desired the accolades of our parents. We would do anything to please them. Pleasing the Father is Packer's third principle. We should live our life always before the Lord, remembering that he sees everything we do and hears everything we say. He is ever present in our day-to-day. This is not an excuse to live obnoxiously pious lives. It is, rather, a perspective we carry as we interact with our families and friends and coworkers. How do we treat them? How do we serve them? How do we speak to them?

Think about what it would mean if, as members of the church, we viewed one another as brothers and sisters, God's children. The "body of Christ" metaphor Paul sets forth in his letters is a great metaphor for how the church functions. But what about how the church lives in relation to one another? What if on Sundays we showed up to see our *brothers and sisters*, not just Tom and Beth from across town? Would intimacy in our gatherings blossom exponentially? Would we start seeing and caring for each other's needs more directly?

The "family of God" motif weaves through Scripture as one of its strongest threads. We see God forming a family at creation, and we see him redeeming his family at the cross. Then we see the church, baptized in fire, and empowered to love. Though we are the body of Christ, each with a specific gifting and purpose, we are foremost the family of God. What kind of revolutionary effect would this view have on our gatherings and our interaction with the world?

As we unravel what it means for us to be children of God, we not only find that there are expectations for being his children, but we also see how living as his children affects our everyday lives. As a mom or dad, sister or brother, coworker or boss, student or athlete, our divinely augmented lives spill out into the world. And though our identities are wrapped in the chrysalis cloak of the eternal Three-in-One, how we express that identity surfaces in the daily. If we peer deeply enough into today, we can see how all the little things crowd in to paint our relationships, both with each other and with God.

———

Easter eve. An outdoor wedding reception. A dad runs too fast after his daughter, so he decides to make it fun and throw himself down the hill, a perfect headfirst grass stain. He slides right by her. She keeps running and throws herself on him. "Wahoo!" her two-year-old voice bellows. The nearby mountain range seems to sing along with her shouts of glee as the girl and the dad play in its shadow.

When the dad catches his breath, he runs, just fast enough, into some old friends, and they talk about life and babies and church and the mountains—how beautiful they sing. The wedding party is detained with photos, so he sips lemonade and nibbles cupcakes and continues to run into his past and present relationships. Quick, nuanced discussions, the kind that corner and reveal.

The dad and his family drive home through the valley along the river; in the graying, the mountains sing. The river echoes the round.

Shuffle, shuffle. Plunge the press. Coffee hot, the morning soars. Hymns on the stereo usher the family on to "the gathering," to church; it's a celebration. The pastor speaks of Thomas, "My Lord, and my God!"

After the body and the blood of the Eucharist, the pastor dismisses the congregation with a benediction: "The grace of the Lord Jesus Christ, and the love of God, and the communion of the Holy Ghost, be with you all. Amen."[18]

The dad wipes his eyes and turns to leave and collides into radiating faces, brothers and sisters united. The soundman bumps into the dad and grabs his baby girl. "I just want to hold her. She's beautiful." The two men smile together; the soundman gets his fill kissing the baby's cheeks and more collisions ensue.

Lunch is a lovely fiasco. Two families, six children, and a floor full of Teddy Grahams; the wait staff serves calmly, patient as the girls scream and run. The adults raise their glasses and toast, "To the celebration! To the resurrection!" Once home, the dad and his family all nap, long and hard. Somewhere in the distance, the mountains sing again.

The Easter weekend emerged from the week and grabbed the dad and his family by the throat. They loved and laughed, fought and cried, and passed through the other side shaped by it all — the run-ins, the discussions, the here, there, and everywhere. But in the post-Easter week, the dad would learn of his mother's new cancer, told to him through his father's tears.

When he is finally able to sit and reflect on it all, life doesn't seem so grand — only tension-filled.

But then he thinks of the Eucharist, how it always seems to break him in half. How, on this Easter Sunday, it reminded him that grace and confession and love all coalesce in the person of Jesus; they are signatures of humanity made beautiful through the divine. The immensity of Jesus' sacrifice wells up and pours from the dad's eyes. So much to take in.

From the Eucharist, his thoughts land somewhere amid the Trinity. He thinks how God runs fast toward humankind, overwhelming everyone with his lavish love. God can't help but love; the dad loves that fact. And those loving fingerprints are everywhere, especially on his family and friends and Easter lunch.

We are social creatures, thinks the dad. *With our loved ones, we dance through this life, though it most often looks like frantic running. And we lean into one another, pushing headfirst to see who will give. Then we fall in a heap amid tears and laughter and pain and joy. God created us this way, and the mystery of the Eucharist completes the puzzle. We are able to love only because he first loved.*

The bees in the dad's back yard love the jasmine blossoms and blueberry buds. They hover, and then climb the popping plumage. They collide and swirl into each other high up into the maples. In a frenzied disappearing act, they abscond into the holly tree, a violent aerial display.

Are they fighting? Lovemaking? Discussing? Laughing? Killing?

We are so much like bees, living the gospel mystery of the Eucharist in the wild collisions of life. And we disappear into death and sex and work and play in a violent showing that rings out, like the mountain song. One another, one another, one another, "our fellowship of kindred minds ... like to that above."[19]

Chapter Eight

TRANSCEND

Reaching beyond Ourselves to Grasp Love

LOVE. LOVE IS THE KEY. LOVE AND FAMILY.
FOR WHAT ARE NIGHT AND DAY, THE SUN,
THE MOON, THE STARS WITHOUT LOVE, AND THOSE
YOU LOVE AROUND YOU? WHAT COULD BE MORE
HOLLOW THAN TO DIE, ALONE, UNLOVED?

– Arthur Burns, The Proposition

And Christ stood before the mob. In front of their jeers and screams he stood, silent. Calling for his execution, the mob grew frenzied. Guards assembled to keep order. Pilate, in private, talked to Jesus.

"So, are you a king or not?"

"You tell me," replied Jesus. "Because I am King, I was born and entered the world so that I could witness to the truth. Everyone who cares for truth, who has any feeling for the truth, recognizes my voice."

"What is truth?" Pilate thought out loud.

And they gathered in the upper room and Jesus broke bread and said ...

"Crucify him!" shouted the mob.

"This is my body." And he took the bread and tore it apart, and blessed it.

"I find nothing wrong with this man," Pilate told them and released Jesus to the mob.

The soldiers, having braided a crown from thorns, thrust it on his head and threw a purple robe over him, and approached him with, "Hail, King of the Jews!"

And he took the cup and blessed it and said, "This is my blood."

They beat Jesus, grinding away any semblance of his humanity. "Prophesy! Who hit you? Prophesy, King of the Jews!"

"Whenever you do this, remember me."

And they pierced his side. Blood and water flowed.

In Christ we find an otherworldly expression of love. His crucifixion model of love offers us a blueprint for building unveneered relationships, as well as providing confidence in our relationship with God. In this crucifixion model, we find vignettes of surrender and personal sacrifice, both stemming from an outrageous humility, both portraying a love that we can imitate in our relationships with one another.

A man marries his college sweetheart. After a while, they have a son. Then another son. Maybe it's because the husband is selfish. Maybe it's because the wife is never satisfied. No matter the reason, the husband begins to cheat on his wife. Over and over. And over. Their whole marriage becomes a lie. To each other, to their family, to their friends, to their church. The wife knows. She has known for some time. One day she finally musters the nerve to say something to the husband. She threatens to leave. The husband, unrepentant, tells her that she doesn't have the courage. He's right.

Years pass and nothing changes. The lies continue. The older son realizes what's happening. He says nothing. He lies. To his family, to his friends. Too ashamed to tell anyone, the wife and the sons and the husband veneer over their family.

The world looks at them and sees nothing unusual. The husband coaches Little League. The wife enjoys a successful career. The sons earn good grades and stay out of trouble. Like every good Southern family, they attend church and listen to *A Prairie Home Companion* on the drive home.

But underneath it all festers the lie that destroys the family. They are too humiliated to have meaningful conversations with each other, too embarrassed to ask for help. They can't keep friends. They eat dinner in front of the TV. They're not honest with each other. They're not honest with the world.

Like this family, everyone endures a certain amount of pain. But we seldom talk about it. No one wants to go around wearing a scarlet letter. So we gloss over it, leaving it unsaid, and the lack of honesty in our lives makes us lonely. We grow dark and bitter, farther removed from God. Despair sets in as true intimacy eludes us. And instead of dealing with our problems, we let them eat away at our insides.

The unsaid – the things in our lives that we keep bottled inside – can, however, be transforming. If we speak the words we normally leave hidden, they become the instruments that help us tear down the walls we hide behind. So speaking the unsaid can begin to turn this family's scenario around for the good.

The husband lovingly shares his thoughts of resentment or anger or hurt to his wife before he looks to an adulterous outlet. He confides in his closest friends his struggle at home. They pray for him, encourage him, and hold him accountable.

The wife doesn't bottle up her feelings. She expresses her disappointments and insecurities and thoughts of inadequacy. Her friendships become places where godly advice is sought and given as other women share how they have worked through their pain.

Together the couple seeks godly counsel. In each other, they begin to see humanity. They see pieces of themselves. The weakness they once felt becomes a point of strength in the relationship, not because the feelings go away, necessarily, but because together they are helping each other.

The couple's trials become guideposts for others. Through the healing process, they learn to share their experiences with hurting friends. Who better to offer counsel through the trials of life than someone who has experienced the same thing? Life's hardships give us a unique perspective. Our relationships grow deeper as we become more honest. "Often, the very part of ourselves that we are most embarrassed by or feel most vulnerable about is the exact gift others need from us," writes Phileena Heuertz in her book *Pilgrimage of a Soul*. "Regardless, embracing these parts of ourselves is crucial to intimacy."[1]

Speaking the unsaid isn't always the verbalizing of our deep feelings. It also takes form in the simple loving expressions capable of breathing new life into our frayed relationships, life-giving expressions with the power to comfort and heal. Phrases like "please forgive me" or "I love you" or "I'm so proud of you" or "you are special to me" can break down our stiff barriers, invite intimacy, and make our brokenness relatable. These actions and words act as stepping-stones that lead us to the deeper healing we all want and need, a deeper love.

All of which require a heavy portion of work. As a result, we oftentimes like the idea of getting close to others rather than the reality of it. Fear stands in our way. We fear rejection. We fear losing the relationship. Afraid of intimacy, our interactions barely scratch the surface, our deeper feelings left alone.

A relationship of intimacy requires courage, the ability to look past uncertainty and see what *could be*. Courage looks beyond our fears and permits us to express feelings that lead us toward intimacy. It requires courage, for example, to confess to your wife that the distance in your relationship is driving you toward depression or even an affair. It requires courage to lovingly tell your friend that she's headed for a fall with her family if she doesn't make serious changes in her work life. It requires courage to admit and to confront. But "the wounds from a lover are worth it."[2]

The idea of courage indicates there may be a risk. Relationally, the risk comes from knowing we may be hurt. Our past indicates that relationships aren't pain free. The daughter who never felt the love of her father, the son who lied, the friend who stopped calling — these types of things fill the baggage that we carry into our newly formed relationships. These experiences can cause us to want to keep our feelings bottled up, to resist trusting someone fully, to hide our true thoughts. If we let them, these wounds can turn us into emotional introverts.

Early in our faith, we learn that to cultivate a deep intimate relationship with Christ, we need to confess and pray to him. We pray to confess the pain we have caused, asking forgiveness of those we have hurt. We pray to share our pain, asking for healing when we experience hurt. As Christ forgives us, we learn to forgive others and ourselves.

When we "speak the unsaid" with our Creator, we experience growth, life, and true relationship: communicating to God from the depths of our being, inching closer and closer to him, becoming familiar with him. In Christ we see fear cast aside and we see healing in our lives and in our relationships, and we find courage in the confidence we have through our relationship with him.

———

In James Joyce's classic *A Portrait of the Artist as a Young Man*, we catch a glimpse of a life committed to forced "religion." Stephen Dedalus, a Jesuit-school student and the main character, at one point experiences religion to the fullest. Or so he thinks. For several pages the author goes into great detail about Stephen's newfound piety. Stephen subjects his body and soul to rigorous discipline, careful not to let any sin or temptation find its way into his soul. As his quest for spiritual perfection mounts, he discovers a power inherent in shunning the desires of the flesh. It appears that Stephen's new religious experience begins to pay dividends for the young man. But then the circumstances turn.

At the zenith of his religious powers, the young spiritual

debutant encounters a "movement of trivial anger in his soul" and some other miniscule sins. He is perplexed at the thought that no matter how righteously he may live, he will not be able to shake them. Guilt plagues his mind and bruises his heart. He wonders if he did something wrong at the beginning of his religious journey. Finally, he takes solace in the fact that his conversion and life of piety *are* sincere, for he has changed himself. "I have amended my life, have I not?" he asks himself.

And so he is convinced.

But in a conversation with his mentoring priest, he is confronted with the ultimate test of his religious belief. The priest asks Stephen to consider the life of a Franciscan. On the one hand, this is the grand prize for all his self-discipline and religious effort. To be flattered by the priest regarding his own leadership qualities and his blameless life is all Stephen had hoped for.

Stephen leaves the conversation and begins the walk back to his parents' house. As he walks, he thinks of himself as a priest, living a life relinquished of his heart's desires, a humble servant of the church. The smell of the church hallways repulses him as he thinks of daily existence in those corridors, how they would *be* his life. And finally, as he gets closer to home, he thinks more upon the invitation of the priest to join their community. But "his soul was not there to hear and greet it [the invitation] and he knew now that the exhortation he had listened to had already fallen into an idle formal tale."

He would not do it. He would not be a priest. "He was destined to learn his own wisdom apart from others or to learn the wisdom of others himself wandering among the snares of the world."[3] Stephen found peace in knowing that the stagnation of the everydayness of the world had won out in his soul. This, to him, was a massive victory.

Like Stephen, we all get an idea of religion, thinking it a grand, powerful way of living, pushing sins out of the way with the flick of our wrist. Eventually, though, we find what Stephen found: that religion by itself holds nothing but dank smells in old church buildings.

A disciplined life that only keeps a list of sins is no life at all. But we can move past the religiosity that keeps us from moving closer to intimate, personal relationship with God.

———

There's a great camping spot in George Washington National Forest called Panther Falls. It's tucked deep in the woods, but if you can borrow a friend's Land Rover, you can make it. The waterfalls, flowing beneath the tall deciduous canopy, tier down the side of the mountains.

At the top of the falls, to the right of the massive boulders jutting from the ground, rests the perfect campsite. Below, the water collects in a deep pool, deep enough to jump into from atop the falls. If you make it to Panther Falls, build your bonfire at dusk and enjoy some hot dogs, cold beverages, and s'mores, then, wait until dark, take off your clothes, and jump from the top of the falls into the dark, freezing-cold pool below. It's not a huge drop, maybe twenty feet. But you will scream like a little girl. You will freeze your eyelids off. And you'll do it over and over and over.

Becoming intimate with God feels a lot like jumping from Panther Falls at night, naked. We stand there contemplating the whole thing. Making sure we jump in the right place so we don't hit the rocks below. A sense of nervous excitement fills our bellies. But if we don't take the first step toward the edge, we miss the point of the trip. We have to jump.

But it's not just the jump that is so invigorating. It's falling from the cliff in the pitch of night, screaming with fright and glee until we hit the water, plummeting from the familiar to the unknown. The cold, the impact, the immediate change to the underwater world—there, time freezes as the exhilaration of the jump courses through our veins. For a moment, the darkness of the underwater world holds us.

People often say that faith is like stepping into the unknown, stepping off a cliff. And for those of us who do jump, we experience significant change. We surface, gasping for air, and then tread silently in the dark water. We are reborn, again – children playing under the watchful eye of the God who whispers to us, "Do it again." And we do; we climb in the darkness, up the cliff, freezing, wet, and fully alive. We go through the same steps, and though we've done it before, a tinge of fear remains and we can't wait for it to overwhelm us. This time we don't step off; we leap. There is darkness. There is the fall. There is the hard impact with the water. But there is now, also, a knowing. Not a knowing in the sense that we fully understand the water or the darkness or the fall but rather a knowing that unfolds. We anticipate the healthy fear of the leap, the excitement of falling into what we can't fully see, and the joy of a new underwater world.

With God, the deeper we plunge, the more he expands. Believing in him is merely the jumping off point, the first step. Intimacy with him feels more like screaming all the way down during the cliff jump and lingering extra long in the underwater world, afraid yet quickened, revealing yet mysterious. We would jump off a thousand cliffs just to feel that sense of aliveness in God. And when, in the risk of our intimacy with him, we realize that his heart burns for us, we can, for that briefest of moments, touch eternity – fully known, expectant to one day fully know.

But too many of us encounter God the way Stephen Dedalus did, as a religious act, devoid of risk, devoid of intimacy, devoid of forgiveness, and devoid of love. Like Stephen, we see how disconnected religion feels in relation to real life, the "disorder, the misrule and confusion" of the day-to-day. So we make the same decision Stephen made: *enough of this calloused piety. I want the real life. I want to make decisions on my own.* Because of a bitter and often misguided religious experience – which is not our own doing – we disregard God in favor of self. And once self is seated upon the throne of our souls, veneer lingers close.

Selfless living seems too painful, we think. So we retreat into our own faith of self. But when we back away from selflessness, we also back away from our relationship with God. They are connected. By understanding one (relationship with God), we are able to live the other (God's language of love). Christ's crucifixion model represents the essence of God's language for living. But we cannot learn the language of sacrifice with comfortable ease. We must approach first through the narrow pathway of humility.

———

Before he went off to Gethsemane to pray, hours before his execution, Jesus met with his closest followers and enjoyed an intimate dinner with them. In John's gospel narrative, we read about their dinner engagement. But laced into the story we read an interesting verse: "Jesus, knowing that the Father had given all things into his hands, and that he had come from God and was going back to God, rose from supper."[4] We recognize the verses that follow this one. They depict Jesus stripping down to his undergarment and washing his disciples' feet, a sobering act in a culture that prized honor and took shame seriously.

In the split second just before he kneels, a *knowing* thought comes into his mind: "The Father had given all things into his hands." But in this moment, Jesus does not stand among them and proclaim his deity, ordering his servants to bow before him. He does not rattle off an elaborate oration or demand a worship ceremony from his disciples. He does not choose to do what we would expect him to do.

He does not do the human-like thing. He does the God-like thing. He kneels.

He kneels knowing that in a few hours, his disciples will fall asleep while in anguish he sweats blood, asking his Father to spare him. He kneels and washes the feet of those who will scatter upon his arrest. He kneels and serves the one who will deny him. Jesus knows this, but he serves anyway.

Again we find ourselves face to face with the deep relational aspect of the triune God. In the foot-washing scene,

Jesus' act of service is not a false humility; he does not patronize the disciples, but rather he models a radical submissiveness. His humility stems from his fierce love for humankind. It comes from his deep wells of mercy that none should perish without finding their way to him. It comes from his overwhelming grace that shows his generous heart, that none should be in utter darkness apart from him. All should be with him in glory.

The apostle Paul reminds us of Christ's humble heart: "Think of yourselves the way Christ Jesus thought of himself. He had equal status with God but didn't think so much of himself that he had to cling to the advantages of that status no matter what....When the time came, he set aside the privileges of deity and took on the status of a slave, became human!... It was an incredibly humbling process. He didn't claim special privileges. Instead, he lived a selfless, obedient life and then died a selfless, obedient death — and the worst kind of death at that — a crucifixion."[5]

Here we uncover the supreme ethic instituted at the cross. It is the ethic of sacrificial love, one person for another, an ethic that considers others first. John the Beloved applies Jesus' sacrificial ethic to each of us when he says that we should lay down our lives for our brother and sister and neighbor. And then we find a compounding element to this love ethic. It is not that we love God; it is that he loved us.

This is pure love, that the I AM would condescend to love us, his creation.

In Ephesians, Paul describes a life that emulates the love of Christ—a progression that begins with humility, continues into sacrifice, and finally expresses itself through a life of love. The love Paul discusses here describes a love that moves into a posture of service as we "walk in *love*, as Christ loved us and *gave himself up* for us, a fragrant offering and sacrifice to God."[6]

It is a rigorous ethic, not warm and fuzzy, nor one of broad doors leading down broad pathways. The ethic of love looks like constant dying—dying to the self, dying to the desires of the heart, dying to whatever hinders our relationship with God and with others.

This is tough for us. Backing away from our own self-promotion is an incredibly difficult proposition. But Jesus' life and death lead us away from ourselves, and as we walk ever closer toward him, we find a surprise. Mysteriously, we find ourselves. Theologian Craig Gay describes the mystery behind losing ourselves to find ourselves when he says that Jesus was talking not about "the rule of Christian religious devotion, but of the rule of existence itself. To truly find ourselves, we *must* lose ourselves to Christ and others."[7]

In the famous Corinthian letter, Paul devotes a whole

chapter to love as the gift found through and because of Christ, a common thread for gospel living. Love "isn't always 'me first.'" It "cares more for others than for self" and "puts up with anything."[8] This progression not only pulls us closer to God but also proves "necessary for true humanity."[9]

When we understand how to love, we are, in reality, understanding how to be human. In his book *The Magnificent Defeat*, Frederick Buechner paints love in beautiful human terms: "The love for equals is a human thing—of friend for friend, brother for brother. It is to love what is loving and lovely. The world smiles. The love for ... those who suffer, for those who are poor, the sick, the failures, the unlovely. This is compassion, and it touches the heart of the world. The love for ... those who succeed where we fail, to rejoice without envy with those who rejoice, the love of the poor for the rich, of the black man for the white man. The world is always bewildered by its saints. [The] love for the one who does not love you but mocks, threatens, and inflicts pain. This is God's love. It conquers the world."[10]

Buechner's words reveal the transcendence in human love through Christ. And we can't help but notice the communal element in his description as well. Community, as most of us discover, challenges our individualistic sensibilities. It forces us beyond ourselves—if it is to work—and wraps us in the life of those we set out to love. There exists an intrinsic accountability in community. It's not enough that we share everything that life throws at us. We must also submit ourselves to the minds and hearts of others. And this is hard. We would rather ramble on by ourselves, answering to no one.

But this only invites an uncomfortable autonomy and emotional distress. The apostle Peter told us to love one another deeply, as brothers and sisters. We cannot do this from the other side of a computer screen or with a one-hour check-in service on Sundays, as the veneered world would have us do. Community, as it is meant in the family of God, does not occur during weekly gatherings around tea and cookies. We must subject ourselves to someone familiar with our quirks and weirdness and secrets, some-one unafraid to speak truth into our lives.

Community emerges out of the same self-abandoned mindset we discovered beneath the whale stars, startling encounters with each other that lead us toward honor of and service to our brothers and sisters. Who are we if not people in loving fellowship, striving toward something greater than ourselves? This is community unveneered: humbling ourselves so that we can serve one another, a daily sacrificing that screams, "I love you."

"If you've gotten anything at all out of following Christ,

if his love has made any difference in your life, if being in a community of the Spirit means anything to you, if you have a heart, if you care—then do me a favor: Agree with each other, love each other, be deep-spirited friends. Don't push your way to the front; don't sweet-talk your way to the top. Put yourself aside, and help others get ahead. Don't be obsessed with getting your own advantage. Forget yourselves long enough to lend a helping hand."[11]

———

Our society has moved past the idea of the transcendent. "*If* there is a God," we say, "what does he care for us?" We tend to see love, especially God's love, through me-colored lenses. We cannot find a place for pain or disappointment or anything that does not serve our desires. And because our view of love plays more like Hollywood's version, we tend to highlight the things that make us feel or look good. "If *I* am cared for, *I* am loved," we say, the focus squarely on ourselves.

But love is so much more than worldly affection. When we reach beyond affection, love opens up. It extends farther than we ever thought possible, like barren trees in wintertime. When we stood beneath them as children, they seemed to reach up into forever like gangly giants creaking in the bitter wind, whistling at the night. Our minds lived in the treetops when we were young, a portal for our imaginations and places of infinite wonder.

And if we are honest, we long for a love like this. An infinite love bigger than us, bigger than our fears and our failings, bigger than losing our jobs or our broken marriages, bigger than our cancer, bigger than our affections, as big as God.

We desire and search for ways to show this kind of love, thinking physical affection its only expression. But physical affection cannot contain love; it only produces a residue, a dim and incomplete rendering of love's true form. "Love is invincible facing danger and death. Passion laughs at the terrors of hell. The fire of love stops at nothing—it sweeps everything before it. Flood waters can't drown love, torrents of rain can't put it out. Love can't be bought, love can't be sold—it's not to be found in the marketplace."[12]

Ironically, it is often the lack of physical affection, from those we desire to be close to, that drives our pursuit for a transcendent love. Because we often associate true love with physical affection, we despair when we do not receive it. Then, when our attempts at true love fail, we struggle with bitterness and resentment, residues of love, by-products of its failure. These strong emotions, however, end up damaging us on the inside, causing us to build up walls to keep the pain from entering again. We give up on our search for an eternal kind of love, happy to "get by." No longer in the treetops of our youth, we abandon the notion of a true and pure and deep kind of love.

But here is where we diverge from God's idea of true love. God's holy and pure love does not float around giving everyone what they want, making them feel good, satisfying random lusts. God's love gives itself up. It endures loss and pain. So many of us struggle with this notion because we view love as a self-fulfilling act rather than a way to be toward God and others. We cannot love without encountering a bit of pain. And the pain comes, in torrents.

The gathering storms forming in this veneered world sidetrack us. It's easier to count our disasters than to fight through the dark clouds rolling across our plastic lives.[13] We often look to a physical love to soothe our wounds. But these frail attempts at a shallow love fumble our relationships into awkward meetings, like teens trying to hold hands for the first time. We try to move, breathe, and live in the feeling of a perpetual first kiss. But the angelic resin dusts off our lips, and we become frustrated, thinking love a sham, the first kiss of innocence lost, the hope of something more, gone. And when we finally give up the chase, we find ourselves sitting, watching "cut-throat busted sunsets ... cold and damp white mornings."[14] We grow weary.

As we climb down from our treetop perspective, we see that life seems to mock love. No one told us the feeling would fade. No one told us we would drink tears instead of wine.

The kids are loaded in; oh, forgot the keys.

The young mom runs in to get them. Dad left for work hours ago. It is just Mom and the kids. Excitement rises as the kids begin the car-ride rituals: yelling, fighting, laughing. But nothing fazes Mom; she smiles through it all. She's put off this appointment for weeks, but now the time has come.

The kids sit, gathered in giddy expectation of Mom's appointment.

"I hope it's another brother."

"I hope it likes doll babies."

The midwife slips into the small room carrying a square box with a long cord attached. The jelly on the tummy – quick happy glances dart among the kids and then at Mom. Over the belly the microphone glides; squishy sounds emanate from the box.

Minutes extend into eternity. Uncertainty gathers in Mom's eyes. More squishy sounds, but no *thump, thump.*

"Oh ..." says the midwife, stuttering. "I'm so sorry."

The kids look to their mom as she wipes her cheeks.

We cannot maintain innocence; life sears with too much calamity and disappointment. So often we are left with clenched fists and betrayed hearts. Our confidence in the goodness of life quickly wanes. Once bitten by loss or betrayal or failure, we shy from engaging too deeply in relationships or new endeavors. The beautiful sheen we once saw in life, that gleam we mistook for our bright tomorrows, dims now. It looks more like a setup. And we will not be played again.

Each time life strikes us with a heavy blow, we back off a bit. We can fail or be rejected only so much. Eventually we break.

But when our affection, in its deep search for passion, turns toward God, then it can be an impetus for deep devotion. Pastor and theologian Jonathan Edwards said that God made affections "the spring of men's actions."[15] It keeps us motivated so that we can kneel to serve others. It is a strong force[16] as we learn to live sacrificially, pouring into the lives of others. Spiritual affection even fuels our wonder, setting us back in the treetops of our innocence. And as we gain confidence in our love with God and others, the hard things we encounter in life take on a new shape.

The bitter Corinthian winter finds Paul restless. For weeks the Christians in Rome have been on his mind. Tonight is no different. The air outside sneaks through the cracks in the walls and the windows and the doors; his apartment is cold. He tends to the fire, more playing with it than anything. As he scours the apartment for a blanket, his mind won't shut off. He lights the candle near his desk and decides to calm his mind by working on his letter to the Roman church.

He has been working with a local writer, dictating his thoughts. But tonight he doesn't bother to send for him. It's too late and too cold. So he digs in with his own hand. He hops onto the hearth of the fireplace, the warm air at his back, the imaginary people of Rome standing below. He raises his arms, "Christ Jesus, who died—more than that ..." He's not talking to anyone, he remembers. He waves off the idea of Christ's dying. "No, no ... he didn't *just* die. He 'was raised to life—is at the right hand of God and is also interceding for us.'"

Paul clutches his cloak in his hands, fighting back tears. He steps down from the hearth and asks quietly, "Who shall separate us from the love of Christ?"[17]

Paul is not simply asking a rhetorical question. He is challenging anyone and anything to thwart Christ's love, the splintered love of a bloody cross. "Shall trouble or hardship or persecution or famine or nakedness or danger or sword?... No, in all these things we are more than conquerors through him who loved us."[18]

But we don't always feel like conquerors, let alone "more than conquerors." There are plenty of times we feel far from God and his love. If we look through the lens of the media, we see a picture of love that never satisfies. More of a "what have you done for me lately" mentality, media-saturated love offers little to our souls, which ache for constancy – something or someone we can always rely on for help or refuge or encouragement.

True love transcends.

God alone transcends space and time, and from him the transcendent elements in our lives find their source. Our society feels dull, filled with things that exist for the sole purpose of taking up space and time. But beyond the prosaic things of society lie the beauties of an arresting rugged creation.

When we take the time to stick our faces into the wildflower blossoms, the intoxicating fragrance points us to the transcendent. When we stop the car along the median of Highway 81 in the foothills of Virginia on the Blue Ridge Parkway and run fast in the sea of red poppies, our spirits soar. The beauty behind their red waving heads lives forever, a glimpse of heaven.

When we visit with friends over dinner, the smell of the bread dancing slowly from the kitchen, the wine sweet, the lively conversation revolving around kids and marriage and music and books, we want time to stand still. Each hour feels like only a minute, an image of the eternal life.

When we catch a hummingbird hovering around our gardens, we're amazed. We point out the window, calling the kids to look; her tiny wings beat ninety times per second, creating a soothing humming sound as she darts up, down, back, forth. The hummingbird leaves us with our heads turned, wondering where she will go next, her delicate beauty pointing us toward the eternal.

Of all these, we recognize there is something – or someone – behind them. And we know that it is God. And when we come across an unveneered person, we see the same thing. We see no guile or worldly deception in them. We see humility. We see a character trait that doesn't point to them, but points to others. We see a servant, living for those whom they encounter. And those they encounter are made greater, their lives elevated, and their status lifted. This is transcendence.

To transcend is the extraordinary, the uncommon. If we desire in our hearts to live lives that imitate Christ, lives stamped with love, then we endeavor to live the transcendent life. True love is anything but common; it is by all means the most extraordinary of things. Created by God, we have his signature in and throughout our very beings; we are his jewels. And so we emerge from our relationships — almost unknowingly — toward the transcendent ethic of love.

We must remember that in all things, love goes beyond the ordinary. Love seeks to serve. Love wakes early on a Saturday, when our eyes burn for lack of sleep, to coach a group of kids. Love makes an inconvenient stop on the side of the road to help a stranger. It sees a child in need of a home and offers one. It goes to a faraway world to carry the gospel message only to be killed on the journey. It serves the poor by creating ways for them to find dignity through work. It rebuilds villages and churches in the face of tribal wars so as to offer hope to a battered people.

Theologian John Stott encourages us to live the ethic of love *like* Christ lived it and *through* Christ as our powering agent and *for* Christ. As we struggle to know how to live, Christ provides an ever-living example for us. And that struggle feels like climbing a mountaintop that keeps getting higher and higher. We keep climbing, hearing his encouraging voice pulling us through the clouds and storm and rain, "Just a bit farther. Climb! You're almost there." And when we come face to face with him, we will at last truly see him and, likewise, make sense of all this life. But we will do it peering through the lenses of perfect heavenly love.

God's language of love is a love stripped of veneer, and there is no pretense or false humility, only the beauty of a bent knee and a bowed head. It is a love that says, "I will wash your feet. You can have my coat. I will help you in your destitution. I will pay your fee. I will give you my last dollar." Love works to pull us away from ourselves, to draw us out of self-service. Love forces us to lift up others, not for our own gain but so that others can find what we have. "In a certain sense," writes philosopher Søren Kierkegaard, the life of the one loving "is completely squandered on the existence of others … in self-sacrifice he is willing to perish … completely and wholly transformed into being simply an active power in the hands of God."[19]

Chapter Nine

VAPOR SUNSHINE

Finding Meaning through Abiding

WHEN HEAVEN MEETS THE EARTH,
WE WILL HAVE NO USE FOR NUMBERS
TO MEASURE WHO WE ARE AND WHAT WE'RE WORTH.

— Sleeping at Last, "Heaven Breaks"

At the end of World War I, many people fell into despair. Infantry bullets shattered the hope of innocence and the belief systems of most people. During the four-year war, sixteen million men and women left home and never returned. They were a generation of people who were told to reach for beauty and love, and that progress would kill the violent instincts of humanity. But the war proved that message a lie.[1]

Humankind, in fact, had not killed the beast instinct with progress and advancement. Instead, the ideology of progress reached out like Tolkien's ring of power and brought new ways to kill through innovative war machines, new ways to corrupt by way of political and economic thirst for power, and new ways to conquer the human spirit. The world found itself twisted around its own greed.

Today, we refer to the writers who emerged from this desolate era as scribes from a lost generation. Whether it was with their themes or characters, these writers began mirroring the reality that watched innocence give way to a world growing ever faster, more powerful, yet without remedies for growing evil and the despair stemming from it.

Chief among these writers, Ernest Hemingway captured the sentiment of the lost generation in his heralded work *The Sun Also Rises*. Hemingway's characters are "almost famous" hack jobs — an almost famous bullfighter, two failed lovers, an almost successful writer. The characters deal with their mediocrity by excessive drinking, and moving from one party to another, from one lover to another. Jake narrates the story. Through him we discover much about this generation. Talking to Georgette, a prostitute he's sharing a drink with, Jake laments:

> "What's the matter with you anyway?"
> "I got hurt in the war," I said.
> "Oh, that dirty war."
> We would probably have gone on and discussed the war and agreed that it was in reality a calamity for civilization, and perhaps would have been better avoided. I was bored enough.[2]

The characters' dialogue drips with a sense of waste. Their struggles parallel our own, allowing us to relate to and resent them all at once. When we finish reading Hemingway's chronicle of these tepid characters, we feel uncomfortable and exhausted.

Time has proven that the disillusioned band of expatriate postwar writers, like Hemingway, weren't the only ones who were lost.[3] We have been lost ever since. And despite efforts to mask our pain and sidestep reality, we can't escape the fact that when we come to the end and meet death, the world will continue.

We are born. We live. We die.

Hemingway seemed to understand the irony of a life wasted. He began his novel with the familiar words from Ecclesiastes: "One generation passeth away, and another generation cometh; but the earth abideth forever ... The sun also riseth ..."

Face to face with meaninglessness, we despair. In our despair, we think it easier to deal with our failures and brokenness by consuming one thing after another. Alcohol. Sex. Whatever. We lose a boyfriend, so we shop. We lose our jobs, so we overeat. We can't talk to our wives anymore, so we Facebook an old flame. At thirty-five, we look back on our lives and wonder what went wrong.

"You need a small tranquilizer," says the Cat in the Hat. "You do, you do indeed." Like the stressed out fish, we sink down in the bowl of this world and drown ourselves with things that make us feel better. Like Hemingway's characters, we live ashamed lives; we take a pill, pound a drink, and put on a happy face. But the inkling of normalcy we feel lasts only a moment. Eventually our pain will catch up with us. Nothing can be hidden forever.

So when we put away the pills and screw the caps back on the bottles, we're faced with the real us. We stand alone, before God and before man, part of a lost generation, and we want to be found. In this moment, we realize that we long for the otherworldly.

———

Everyday life crawls into our beds and whispers, "What's next?" Its smiling voice beckons us, almost pulling us. As we wipe the crusty sleep from our eyes, we smile because we recognize the voice. We remember it from that trip we took to the ocean when we graduated from high school. We felt so alive that day. Life didn't just whisper to us in the morning; it shouted into everything we did.

We remember vivid elements of that trip. Everyone got up early so we could arrive before dawn. We hiked over the dunes in the morning twilight. We made our way down the path toward the sound. Was it the sound of the waves we heard, or was it the sound of life?

And there we stood. While the waves crashed on our feet, memories jumped out of our conversations and painted our four years together—what a strange and wonderful dance. *I never want to get old. I love this*, we thought.

You know that voice too. That's the voice you hear now as you brush your teeth in the morning. It's the voice that you love to hear and always want to follow. But lately, for you, the voice sounds more like a whisper. You know you're sidetracked with all the things filling your day, but you're confident that tomorrow the voice will return, stronger than ever. But does tomorrow ever come? Is the voice gone?

Too often the society that humankind created for itself drowns the voice of vitality with "humdrum, humdrum." The everyday turns passé, and slowly we sink into the mediocre script that we mistake for life. Life's inevitable decay from sublime to the ordinary can drive many of us toward veneer. We see signs every day that remind us life is "but a breath,"[4] just a vapor. Our days dissolve before us and vanish in the rearview mirror. Life slips from our grasp quicker than we ever thought possible, and in a hasty attempt to regain that sunrise morning at the beach with our friends, we fabricate an existence bent on inflated experiences.

What was it about that sunrise experience with our friends from high school, the effervescence of life clinging to the very words everyone spoke? In that moment, we were known by our friends. A great and unmistakable calming shot our hearts forward in time, and everything looked perfect. Why can't it all be perfect? We didn't worry that day about being accepted by our friends. We were all just friends. And friendship goes beyond acceptance and exists somewhere in the kingdom of heaven, doesn't it?

Friendship feels a lot like our mother's embrace from when we were five. That embrace dripped with a love so deep and so wide that it enveloped our entire world. It captured us in a moment we wished would never end.

But we're older now, and many of those memories seem naïve. Sometimes we look on them with disdain. Life is different now; it feels different now. A sense of waste, at times, overwhelms us all. T. S. Eliot's words feel right:

> We are the hollow men
> We are the stuffed men
> Leaning together
> Headpiece filled with straw. Alas!
>
> Shape without form, shade without colour,
> Paralysed force, gesture without motion.[5]

Society's structure forces us to play its game: do this, look like this, accomplish this, and you will be accepted. And because we want so much for this sense of waste to go away, we acquiesce to society's rules and regulations. In five years, we'll be head of our department or we'll have our graduate degree or we'll own the company. In five years, we will embody what it means, what it takes, to be accepted; which is really just another way to say we'll have achieved success according to the world's standards.

As we bend to societal pressure, we realize the truth in what King Solomon, the Teacher in Ecclesiastes, wrote: "Meaningless, meaningless. Everything is meaningless." But this cannot be the language of God, can it? Meaninglessness? How can we get past the sense of waste that pervades the world? How can we remain in the world, yet move farther into God's purpose for life?

———

In the Teacher's time, society viewed the gathering of wealth and power as means to gain personal worth. This common secular mindset sounds familiar; our society views the "end-all" in the same fashion. This secularism says, "We don't need God for anything. We're doing fine on our own." So Ecclesiastes' strong words about wealth, wisdom, power, and toil as meaninglessness flew in the face of what most — during that time — held as true.

But even in the ancient world people felt the void left

by such pursuits. Their despondency led to an outgrowth of "pessimism literature" that gained popularity during the Teacher's time. Philosophers saw all the wealth and power accumulated by kings and had one question: so what? In many cases, some of the great thinkers came to the lurid conclusion that only death or even suicide was the answer to life's meaninglessness. So Ecclesiastes was not uncommon in its overall questioning tone; it spoke directly into the spirit of the day.[6]

But here is where the Teacher's sentiments eventually separate from the ancient pessimistic literature. Early in the book, the Teacher changes his tone from blaming God for everything to seeing God *in* everything: "So I *decided*," writes the Teacher, "there is nothing better than to enjoy food and drink and to find satisfaction in work. Then I *realized* that these pleasures are from the hand of God. For who can eat or enjoy anything apart from him?"[7]

Our things are nice—our houses, our flat screens, and our cars. But in the end, the vapor-things of this world will vanish. When it does, the only thing that will matter is our relationship with God and how that relationship played out in our lives. Having realized this himself, the Teacher reminds us to keep a healthy perspective on these pursuits.

The Teacher concludes, "Fear God and obey his commands, for this is everyone's duty."[8] He boils everything down to the simplicity of this final proverb. We fear him, or revere him, because he's the all-knowing, all-caring, all-everything, whale-star-creating God. When we're uneasy about our future, he provides peace because we trust the one who governs it. Fear God: trust in his sovereign and holy nature that this life consists of more than a chasing after vapor.

We want to revere him. We want to be known by him, to be seen by him for who we really are, stripped of our veneer. We don't want the meaninglessness of the world; we want the real of the eternal.

This is the dead land, this is the cactus land.[9]
And in this wasteland we've lost our identity.
Between the conception and the creation ... falls the shadow.[10]
So we cry out:

Scrub away my guilt, soak out my sins in your laundry. I know how bad I've been; my sins are staring me down. You're the One I've violated, and you've seen it all, seen the full extent of my evil.

You have all the facts before you; whatever you decide about me is fair. I've been out of step with you for a long time, in the wrong since before I was born. What you're after is truth from the inside out. Enter me, then; conceive a new, true life. Soak me in your laundry and I'll come out clean, scrub me and I'll have a snow-white life.

Tune me in to foot-tapping songs, set these once-broken bones to dancing. Don't look too close for blemishes; give me a clean bill of health. God, make a fresh start in me, shape a Genesis week from the chaos of my life.

Don't throw me out with the trash, or fail to breathe holiness in me. Bring me back from gray exile, put a fresh wind in my sails! Commute my death sentence, God, my salvation God, and I'll sing anthems to your life-giving ways.

I went down to the very bottoms of the mountains; the gates of the netherworld barred me in forever; but you brought me up from the Pit, O Lord, my God.

I'll never forget the trouble, the utter lostness, the taste of ashes, the poison I've swallowed. I remember it all — oh, how well I remember — the feeling of hitting the bottom. But there's one other thing I remember, and remembering, I keep a grip on hope.

And God replies to our cry,

I am the root and the descendant of David, the bright morning star! Let the one who is thirsty come; let the one who wants it take the water of life free of charge.

I am the light of the world. If you follow me, you won't have to walk in darkness, because you will have the light that leads to life.

Are you tired? Worn out? Burned out on religion? Come to me. Get away with me and you'll recover your life. I'll show you how to take a real rest.

Walk with me and work with me — watch how I do it. Learn the unforced rhythms of grace. I won't lay anything heavy or ill-fitting on you. Keep company with me and you'll learn to live freely and lightly.

Those who wait upon me get fresh strength. They spread their wings and soar like eagles. They run and don't get tired, they walk and don't lag behind.[11]

———

In our tragic distance from God — our separatedness — our view of life distorts. But we also sense something more; we *know* there is something more. The Teacher tells us that God "has planted eternity in the human heart, but even so, people cannot see the whole scope of God's work from beginning to end."[12] And so we live in the tension of knowing that eternity opens up before us, and yet each morning the television news churns out more stories of human brokenness. Chasing eternity is like chasing your shadow on a bike: you pedal as fast as you can, you can see it on the ground before you, but you can't grasp it — that is our lot in this life.

Our separatedness, however, diminishes as Christ's renewal begins to shape our life. Christ, as the divine God-man, quickens our eternal perspective. Through him we see traces of eternity in our relationships and even our work and our pleasures, pointing us toward something else: the Other.

The Other represents God and his transcendent fingerprint upon all that we do in this life. But many of us are professional compartmentalizers; we make it our job to separate spiritual things from real life. We think God and transcendence and all those gooey words don't mean anything in the everyday grind. If that is our view, then we tie ourselves to nothing more than the stop-and-go of traffic and paychecks.

When we happen upon the whale stars and encounter the Other, we think, *That can't happen in the "real" world*, as if the Durango night sky exists only for vacationers and hippie hikers.

But God's otherness smothers all of life, not just the epic wonder of the untamed Four Corners area. The whale stars represent literal stars, but they can also represent you and your dad sitting down and hashing out the last few disagreements, or you and your best friends volunteering at a local charity. As we move out into the new frontier of our faith, we change. We begin to see the whale stars everywhere, not just the remote corners of our life. The world becomes a new place as we stumble into the bright shadow of his otherness.[13] We see things differently. We move away from our idol-filled world and fall deeper in love with the real, living, intimate God. This is where he calls everyone.

———

On September 11, 2001, at 8:46 a.m., American Airlines Flight 11 crashed into the north tower of New York City's World Trade Center, and in the blink of an eye, the world changed. Seventeen minutes later, United Airlines Flight 175 hit the south tower. During the next sixty minutes, a plane flew into the Pentagon in Washington, D.C., and another crashed in the farmland of western Pennsylvania.

The generation before ours had their "date which will live in infamy," as President Franklin D. Roosevelt called it, when the Japanese attacked Pearl Harbor. Now we had ours. No one will forget the scenes played over and over on television: the smoke, the crumbling towers, the falling people, the tears, the confusion, the "missing" posters, the makeshift memorials. On that day, it seemed like the end was finally here. The world was over.

Like most of us, Jack Murray felt the weight of the world ending. From the roof of his Manhattan apartment, he could see the smoke billowing into the heavens and thought, *The world is going to come to an end ... Today's the last day I am alive.* So he headed down to the local pub. If this was his last day, then he was going to drink a couple of cold ones with friends and watch the whole thing unfold on CNN.

But as Jack sat there wrestling with the gravity of the moment, his plans changed. Knowing Jack was a welder, one of the pub owners came over and convinced him to go help the people suffering down at the crash site. Jack agreed and became one of the first twenty steel burners to go into the site and work at cutting away debris.

As Jack worked—the rubble and smoke and dust hitting him in the face—he came to a profound realization. "I had this thought that I was standing on this gigantic funeral pyre going into the earth," he recalls. "I realized I was probably breathing in the ashen remains of some of the people. It was kind of like a communion for me."[14]

On that September day, life changed for most of us. If only for a while, our perspective on what matters in life crystallized. We had no choice. Many lost their jobs. Many lost their friends. Many lost sons and daughters, moms and dads.

By some estimates, on the Sunday after the attacks, more than half of the adult population of the United States attended some sort of religious service.[15] As a nation, we searched for answers, looked for hope, and filled the pews of the country for a chance to find both.

Soon, for those not directly impacted by the event, things went back to a sense of normalcy. We began to work and make money and collect things. But looking back, we remember our search. We remember what we longed for during that period. And now, living in a world of home foreclosures and high unemployment rates, we wonder what we would have found if we had kept looking.

For many of us, the changing tide of the economy heaves us into the search for meaning, for the eternal. And in this search, we find Jesus having dinner with his closest friends hours before his death. During that dinner, we see a mysterious breaking of bread and drinking of wine. Two thousand years later, he calls us to that same dinner, in remembrance of him. And so we partake. The sacrament beckons us into the blessedness of following after him. "I am the true vine," he says. And we are his branches. "Abide in Me, and I in you."[16]

When we partake of Christ through the bread and the

cup, it's as though we inhale him into our very being, carrying him around with us, his presence powering our lives. He says that if we don't abide in him, we will be like the branches that don't produce any fruit; they're cut away and burned, useless, meaningless.

Apart from Christ, the world *is* meaningless. Apart from Jesus, we are nothing. We can do nothing. "Abide in me," he says. "See the world from a new perspective." But how do we abide?

———

Kierkegaard helps us understand what it means to abide. He tells the story of a couple in love. The girl, seeing that her relationship with her beloved could be facing obstacles, asks him to wait for her. And he does.

But what happens if the circumstances strain, making the wait too long? What if her beloved moves on? Kierkegaard says that when we cease to be loving, we were never loving in the first place. "For love abides."[17]

By telling the disciples (and us) to abide, Jesus is telling them to wait *in* him. Jesus says to them, "If you keep my commandments, you will abide in my love ... this is my commandment, that you love one another as I have loved you."[18]

So obedience is central to the abiding life. We're first

to obey the double commandment: love God and love one another. As we obey these two commands, we cultivate devotion and sacrifice. These are the building blocks of intimacy. Most of us understand devotion, but sacrifice is harder for us because of its demands.

In John the Beloved's gospel, we find the concept of sacrifice communicated in Jesus' discussion with his disciples as he calls them friends: "Greater love has no one than this: to lay down one's life for one's friends. You are my friends if you do what I command. *You* are my friends ... I no longer call you servants,"[19] says Jesus.

For John's Jewish readers, this distinction mattered. Servants, though loyal in relationships with their masters, didn't share intimately with them. And the rabbis regarded only Abraham and Moses as God's friends. What's more, Jewish teaching differed from the Greco-Roman view on dying for one's friend or a family member. Rabbi Akiba, who was not far removed from John's time, said, "One's own life took precedence over another's."[20]

John's Greek audience, however, would have appreciated the idea of dying for a friend. Their culture valued the heroism, loyalty, and intimacy inherent in friendship. To them, dying for a friend was the ultimate expression of a deep relationship. So Jesus' words to his disciples here were exceptional. To them, being a friend of God carried great significance. And as Jews in a Greek society, their cultural (Hebrew) understanding of friendship would have sweetened the words.[21]

In this discussion of friendship and dying, we see sacrifice as a by-product of intimacy. In order for a person to make the ultimate sacrifice for another, a depth of love must exist. Jesus had it with his disciples, and he has it with us because he is our Creator and laid down his life to reestablish a way for us to connect with him, to be intimate with him.

If we want to get to the heart of abiding, we must cultivate intimacy, and intimacy begins with connectivity. To connect means to form a relationship. Connecting to another person, to our friends and family, requires heroic effort for sure, especially in an age of trite "friend requests." But we need to do more than simply make connections; we need to stay connected. The vine in Jesus' analogy reveals the depth to which our intimacy must run. When we become estranged in our relationships, they wither, like the branches on the vine.

Abiding is staying connected with God and others, not losing the bond that created the deep relationship. Staying connected to God requires us to seek him in his Word and to listen for him throughout our day. Think through the actual times of quiet and stillness in your day. Now think through the times of organized chaos and busyness and overall insanity. It's the same for all of us. Staying connected with God in today's veneered world might mean waking up an hour earlier than normal to sit in silence. It might mean setting up monthly spiritual retreats, finding a place of solitude and just being.

Relationships, like the branch to the vine, need attending and patience and even pruning. Relationships demand our time and attention. They demand selfless interaction. When we neglect our relationships, as when we neglect the growing vine, disease and decay settle in. We become distant from one another, quick to seat resentment in our hearts, quick to allow bitterness to seep into our relational roots. And we struggle to separate our relational failings on earth with our ideas about God. If we're not careful, estrangement from God can settle in, and life can take on a cold pragmatism. Birth and death, gain and loss — we find ourselves sitting with the ancient pessimists eating and drinking, looking toward death.

But this is where the immensity of Jesus overwhelms the world. In a conversation with a Samaritan woman, Jesus refers to himself as "living water," a life-giving source, satisfying the divine thirst inside everyone. As the world spins toward oblivion, raging on in an ever-echoing toast to "get all you can," Jesus himself flows into our lives, misting our souls with his presence. He surges deep into our anxious thoughts and notions, giving life. We can hear the language of God in these living waters, the mysterious language coursing through our dry insides. What if we would allow ourselves to be caught in his flash flood of life? Would we swim for dry land, or allow him to carry us farther into himself? If we allow him to carry us into himself, we discover his life-giving waters never dry. These waters power us, enabling us to live always abiding, even drowning, in him.

The overwhelming flood that is Jesus produces a spiritual crop in us from which characteristics like patience grow. Like the lover waiting for her beloved, we learn to wait for him. Perseverance springs forth as well, made hardy from life's tumult, pushing us to cling to the vine. Our roots deepen, giving us the strength to live as an expression of him. We are forever connected to him, a connection that produces a life that climbs and weaves and blossoms, one that offers the fragrance of divine intimacy.

———

The abiding life stems from obeying God's commandments and obeying his voice. His voice sounds like the unrelenting voice inside your head that tells you to do the unexpected. And the more you hear it and think about it, the more you wonder if it makes sense.

It's the voice that softly tells you that your job is suffocating your soul and that you should replace it with the unknown. Sure, the hefty paycheck and executive position give you a sense of accomplishment and respect and power. But at home, your relationships break apart and you feel ever distant from those you love. As it turns out, "What is good for the modern economy, it seems, is not necessarily very good for the soul."[22]

But what are you supposed to do? Quit your job and find one that pays less but allows you more time at home? What would the world think? Your parents? Your friends? Your whole life, you've been told to find security, to find a good job, make money, save for your future, build your resume, buy a nice house, and drive a nice car.

Ignoring the voice seems like a comfortable alternative. You could stay in control. But to follow the voice would be to answer the call of the wild, and following the voice could change you, and generations after you, forever.

We hear this voice repeating throughout life, asking us to give of ourselves in various ways. Sometimes it's our jobs that haunt us, past relationships that need closure and forgiveness, little secrets that keep us up at night. But to listen to the voice means giving up control, and we don't like that. The uncertainty seems too overwhelming.

In the most famous sermon ever preached, Jesus says to the crowd, "What I am trying to do here is to get you to relax, to not be so preoccupied with *getting*, so you can respond to God's *giving*. People who don't know God and the way he works fuss over these things, but you know both God and how he works."[23]

As we stay connected to the Vine, we realize that our needs are met. The Vine is our source. The Vine is our sustenance.

"Seek first the kingdom of God and his righteousness," Jesus continues, "and all these things will be added to you."[24] In seeking him, we find blessing. But not the kind of blessing we sought before we learned how to abide. It's not a material blessing at all but rather the blessedness of finding him. The desires for worldly things and success fade away, replaced by the spiritual blessings of the "seek first."

Jesus concludes, "Give your entire attention to what God is doing right now, and don't get worked up about what may or may not happen tomorrow. God will help you deal with whatever hard things come up when the time comes."[25]

Listening to God doesn't always sound like a secure

choice; it's entirely counter to society. It's a life that's spent suppressing our earthly desires and replacing them with the eternal desires of God, a life spent out of our control but firmly in his. He will provide. He will help you with all that life throws at you. Tomorrow is not our concern. In abiding, we find confidence. In abiding, we find relationship. In abiding, we find power. In abiding, we find grace.

Chapter Ten

END VENEER

Pursuing the Uncommon Way

THE LIFE OF SENSATION IS THE LIFE OF GREED;
IT REQUIRES MORE AND MORE. THE LIFE
OF THE SPIRIT REQUIRES LESS AND LESS;
TIME IS AMPLE AND ITS PASSAGE SWEET.

— *Annie Dillard,* The Writing Life

The dull roar of anticipation exploded into a raucous cry. The merchants, frantic, rushed their carts out of the way. Shop owners shut their windows and locked their doors. People ran toward the edge of the street pushing their way to a better view. The procession of priests closed in on the square. The trumpet blasts ricocheting off the city walls propelled the moment.

A farmer made his way to the front of the crowd and could see *it* clearly, right in front of him. The ark was home at last. David, the king, had brought it back. The procession halted as David raised his hand. The frenzied celebration paused. In the silence, the king shouted, "Israel, put your hope in the LORD both now and forevermore!"[1] The crowd cheered. The trumpets blared. The people danced. The farmer danced. The king danced and drank and sang with them. He "danced before Jehovah with all his might."[2] The great procession ended. The farmer returned to his home, the king to his palace.

Sweaty and tired from the long day's march and celebration, David drew some water to clean his face. As he leaned over the sink, he heard Michal, his wife, enter the chamber.

He turned and found her pacing back and forth. He said nothing. She stopped pacing and faced him. "The way you acted today, in the streets, at the party—that is not acceptable behavior for a king," she explained. "The people don't need to see you romping. I mean, you're their king …" she trailed off.

After he dried his face and laid the towel down, he looked at her. He saw the disappointment in her eyes. But David knew there was more to consider than the expectations of those around him. He must consider *himself*—the person, the child, who stood before God. He knew that he could not afford to live by others' standards. He knew his place in the gaze of God.

So the confident king, tired and wanting to go to bed, did what most of us do not. He took the hard road. He gave the answer that he knew could cause a fight and days of discussion and mending and sleeping on the couch.

"I didn't dance to please you or the people," he said, moving toward her. "I don't care about man's approval. How can I when I stand in the presence of God?" His voice rose. "I act crazy, but for him. And I will dance and I will drink and I will lose all dignity if I have to! I don't care who sees. If I dance naked before my God, what is that to you or anyone?"

Michal, shocked, ran out of the room. David stood alone.

Later, David wrote, "O Lord, you have searched me and known me!... For you formed my inward parts ... I praise you, for I am fearfully and wonderfully made. Wonderful are your works; my soul knows it very well."[3] David *knew* God. And from knowing God, wisdom and confidence flourished in his life. But how did David reach the point where he could dance undignified in front of the whole nation of Israel, not caring what anyone thought?

David's life intrigues and confuses us. We know his baggage: adulterer, conspirator, and murderer. And we know his fame: giant killer, poet, great strategist, and king. But we don't understand how someone with such a color-ful and even wild past—how a king could dance in front of the masses the way he did—can still be called a man after God's own heart.[4]

David endeavored to move the ark once before, but it didn't end well. The sloppy attempt cost Uzzah his life after he placed his hand on the ark to keep it from falling. David, angry and fearful, stopped the procession immediately. Unwilling to continue in folly, David left the ark nearby with Obed-edom the Gittite for three months. David didn't understand why he was unable to return the ark to the city of David at first. But during the three months the ark was with Obed-edom, David realized that he "failed to ask God how to move it properly."[5]

David's second attempt to move the ark, however, resulted in a worshipful celebration with the brazen king dancing undignified in public. Why the sudden shift in confidence? Why the blatant disregard for what anyone else thought of him, including his wife?

When we pursue the things that God pursues, when our passions align with his, we become people after God's heart. When David realized his error, finally understanding God's protocol for moving his ark, he took it seriously. He pursued God's instruction with abandon, making sure that nothing was overlooked. There's a passage in the Old Testament that reveals how serious David was about moving the ark correctly, describing in tremendous detail the pains David took to do what God commanded. And when success followed, when the ark entered the city, David danced; he pleased God.

David's baggage proves how much his heart was like ours. But when David had the chance to turn from selfish or errant ways, when he had the chance to make something right, he took it. He wanted what God wanted. What do we want?

Knowing and pursuing God isn't about being perfect.

It's about realizing we aren't perfect and yet striving to follow after God with our very souls – to want what God wants.[6] Remember when Nathan confronted David about Bathsheeba? "You are the man, David!" he declared.[7] David didn't make petty excuses; he tore of his clothes and wept in shame, begging forgiveness, an adulterer exposed, a repentant spirit, a man after God's heart.

The mystery of David's heart for God reveals the origin of David's confidence to dance with all his might. When we live, humbly pursuing God's heart, the desires of the world fade. Like David, we stop caring about other people's reactions and focus our efforts on glorifying God in everything we do. "The Lord does not see as mortals see," writes Samuel the prophet, "they look on the outward appearance, but the Lord looks on the heart."[8] Our confidence, then, should manifest itself in our knowledge that God sees past the patina of our lives – our failures, our brokenness, our embarrassments – and into our souls. That's his main concern. Are we doing what we can to cultivate our souls through our pursuit of God?

David's times of prideful self-serving were always followed by awareness of the sin and repentance. "Have mercy on me, O God, according to your unfailing love ... God, make a fresh start in me, shape a Genesis week from the chaos of my life."[9] Stripping our veneers sounds like the cry of a broken king asking for a new beginning. The fresh start we see in David corrects his relationship with God at the heart level, which leads to proper action.

As in David's life, change in our lives should happen on two levels – the unseen (outer actions) and the seen (inner heart). And as philosopher Dallas Willard reminds us, our actions do not emerge out of thin air. They are formed, rather, by a transforming of the "inner life of the soul." Once this transformation happens, our actions follow, not the reverse.[10] If you don't change the unseen, you will not be able to sustain the seen changes.

In working toward the unseen changes, we find the idea of *renewals*. In the New Testament the word *rewewal* (*anakainosis*) is found only twice, both written by the apostle Paul. One of the two verses is Romans 12:2, where Paul issues an urgent and essential command to Christians. He says don't be conformed by this present age; rather change your form – be a transformed person – by renewing your way of thinking.[11]

Paul considered the mind to be the battleground for the soul and a central hub for spiritual development. In Paul's letter to the Ephesians, he encourages the members of the church to have a different mindset from that of the rest of society. He describes the society in Ephesus as having darkened understanding and futility of mind. Both result in alienation from God. Their callous inner self produces aimlessness in their physical lives as well. Since their hearts have gone cold toward God, the world and its pursuits are all that remain. Paul refers to these pursuits as sensuality and a lust for all kinds of impurity.

Every day, we encounter the spirit of this present age and, if we aren't careful, it will shape the way we think, and subsequently the way we act. So we must take great care of our minds with regard to what we allow to shape our thinking. In both letters, to the Ephesians and to the Romans, Paul urges Christians to a different kind of mind, one shaped by God.

Pursue renewal in your relationship with God and in your personal relationships. Relationships grow only when you spend time cultivating them. Our vertical relationship with God affects our horizontal relationships with our friends, family, coworkers, and peers. So start with the vertical.

The psalmist says happy is the person who delights in God's laws, who spends time contemplating the ways of God. Initiating renewal in your relationship with God can be as simple as spending time in quiet prayerful reflection on his Word, listening to his voice speaking to your spirit.

Take time to reflect on a verse or a passage of Scripture and ask God to open his Word to you. Our culture does not value reflection. We think we need to be active in order to accomplish great things. But great things begin in the "soil of reflection."[12] It is the time involved in reflection that enables growth.

So take your time with God. Dive into the Psalms and let the words wash over you. Silently pray them and listen for God's voice. David wrote,

> Make me understand the way of your precepts,
> and I will meditate on your wondrous works.
> My soul melts away for sorrow;
> strengthen me according to your word!
> Put false ways far from me
> and graciously teach me your law![13]

As Oswald Chambers reminds us, we should go to God in order to hear from him first, not to ask of him. Don't be overwhelmed by your uncertainty of how to communicate with God. Offer yourself as an open vessel, and he will speak to your heart.

Remember, Jesus said that he and the Father are one. If you need a personal face for God, then pursue Jesus.[14] He calls you friend, so go to him as such. Retreat to a quiet place; talk to him like you would with your best friend during a venting session. Give yourself permission to engage in honest confession with him. Lay your baggage before him, clean your spiritual slate. Relational renewal with God finds the Christian in the prostrate position of confession and repentance.

John the Beloved says when we confess our specific sins to God, we can live in the assurance of God's forgiving nature, for God delights in showing unfailing love. And, significant to our pursuit of a renewed relationship, John says that when we confess, we invite fellowship with God.

We can apply confession and reflection to our horizontal relationships with people as well. Just as you begin cultivating times of quiet reflection on God's Word and his voice, do the same in your personal relationships. The idea here is to spend meaningful time with them. Seek others out; plan times that allow for discussion and encouragement. Invite them to share; probe deeper than the normal talk of schedules and television shows. Listen to their hurts. Hear their needs. The apostle Peter encourages Christians to "love one another deeply, from the heart," to love like brothers.[15] Do your utmost to be a loving brother or sister in your relationships.

Confession will invite fellowship in your personal relationships too. The Eucharist is a great time to practice confession. If your church performs the Eucharist on a regular basis, take advantage of that time to seek out an estranged friend. Pull your spouse aside and confess specific things you know have caused rifts in your relationship during the week.

"Make this your common practice," writes James. "Confess your sins to each other and pray for each other so that you can live together whole and healed. The prayer of a person living right with God is something powerful to be reckoned with."[16]

Pursue renewal of your life purpose. We've learned that the language of culture tries to convince us that we should pursue success and fame, outward beauty, and the accumulation of things as means to gauge our purpose in life. But these things center on you, making you look good and feel good. God did not create humanity so it could lose itself in these false pursuits. We derive our purpose in life by being rightly related to God and understanding our position before him. Only from this vantage point will life make sense.

God says, "Before I formed you in the womb I knew you, and before you were born I consecrated you."[17] He knows each one of us, appoints us to do certain things and empowers us to do it. But he does this to glorify himself.

"For from him and through him and to him are all things. To him be glory forever. Amen."[18] Even when Jesus was on this earth, he said that his purpose was to do God's will.

The next step, then, is to evaluate yourself — your job, your societal pursuits, your studies. Is your direction in life representative of a child of God living to glorify him in everything? It's easy to convince ourselves that because things are working out financially or socially, we are living blessed lives. That may be the case. But keep in mind that those are measurements the world uses. God's measurements look much different: if you want to find your life, you should lose it; narrow is the way to God; if you want to be great, you must be the servant of all.

To renew our life's purpose, we need to flip it on its head. Our quest for purpose should not be focused on figuring out what we're doing in this life with regard to schooling, career, or vocation. It should be focused on the assurance that God knows us, has a task for us, and will empower us to do it for his glory. Ask yourself, How can I best glorify God? And then go and do it.

Pursue renewal in your reverence for God by countering idol worship. Stop raising the world's brands, cultural icons, and vain pursuits as your personal idols. It's easy to allow these things to distract you from God. "People knew God perfectly well," writes Paul, "but when they didn't treat him like God, refusing to worship him, they trivialized themselves into silliness and confusion so that there was neither sense nor direction left in their lives.... They traded the glory of God who holds the whole world in his hands for cheap figurines you can buy at any roadside stand."[19]

Pastor Timothy Keller says that idol worship stems from our motivations. It's not just that we hoist up cheap figurines; it's also the "why" behind it. He says we are unwilling to glorify God and "choose created things as gods."[20] This results in a life of veneer.

To counter idol worship and renew our view of God as reverent and deserving of all glory, we need to wash away the societal scales blinding our eyes. We need to approach him once again as children. G. K. Chesterton says that the materialism of the world dupes us all into false assumptions. Because society inundates us with images and ideas that change almost every second, we think that anything not moving fast must be dead.

Chesterton then points us to children's immense love of repetition. "Because children have abounding vitality, because they are in spirit fierce and free, therefore they want things repeated and unchanged. They always say, 'Do it again'; and grown-up people are not strong enough to exult in the monotony."[21] Do we raise up the world's trinkets and power and fame because they keep us moving along, satisfying some immediate need? Perhaps we fail in revering God because we've moved on to deities that upload, are customizable, and are centered on ourselves.

"It may be that He [God] has the eternal appetite of infancy," continues Chesterton, "for we have sinned and grown old, and our Father is younger than we."[22] Jesus tells us that if we want to come to him, we need to be childlike. Children view their parents with a tremendous amount of trust, an appropriate amount of fear, and sheer delight. To renew reverence toward God, we need to first confront, name, and rid our lives of personal idols. Second, we need to think like children again. We need to shout at the sky when we see the sunrise, "Do it again, God!" We need to find our knees more often as we approach him with appropriate honor and respect. And we need to regain our delight in him as Lord, Creator, and Father.

Pursue renewal in what and in whom you find reliance. Reliance reveals our hearts as trusting or not trusting. If we rely upon the progress of society to keep us safe, well fed, sheltered, and wealthy, then we, in essence, are saying that society offers steadfastness in its offerings. When we hold this mindset, we inevitably move God to the margins. But the psalmist reminds us, "Those who know your name trust in you, for you, LORD, have never forsaken those who seek you."[23]

In a beautiful passage in the book of Matthew, Jesus helps us gain perspective on what really matters in life. He reminds us that there's more to life than worrying about what we will eat or what we will wear or where we will live. He scoffs at those who rely on the world for confidence regarding their outward appearance or material sustenance. "Look at the birds," he says, "free and unfettered, not tied down to a job description, careless in the care of God. And you count far more to him than birds.... All this time and money wasted on fashion – do you think it makes that much difference? Instead of looking at the fashions, walk out into the fields and look at the wildflowers. They never primp or shop, but have you ever seen color and design quite like it?...If God gives such attention to the appearance of wildflowers – most of which are never even seen – don't you think he'll attend to you, take pride in you, do his best for you?"[24]

We're an anxious bunch. Doesn't it seem like we're always preoccupied with things of minor consequence? To renew our reliance on God, we need to be about his business. We can't do this if we're flitting around trying to secure our future.

Pursue renewal as a member of God's family, the church. The church should offer an unending source of hope in the shallow world of veneer. In order to offer hope to society, the church leadership and parishioners should focus on three main areas: the church's purpose both corporately and personally, our passion and devotion for God's Word both corporately and personally, and our commitment to discipleship within the church and the community. Many books have been written on these topics, but what follows should stir us to consider our own roles within the church body and to move us toward prayerful consideration for the church.

To see the beauty of the church, we can look at its purpose. Most will agree that the corporate purpose of the church is to edify and equip the saints to preach the gospel – through their lives, or otherwise – and to make disciples. This can serve as our starting point for discerning the methods we should use as the church. More specifically, we see the beauty of the church in what it provides to its congregants and to all humanity: the hands and feet of Christ that work throughout the world, equipping of saints to do the work of Christ, edification of saints, devotion to the brethren, the body and blood of Christ taken together and the accountability that comes through this sacrament, and the baptism of new believers.

The early Christians, for example, gathered on Sundays for what they referred to as Little Easter celebrations, to worship God by reading Scriptures, teaching from one or more pastors or elders, community prayer, taking the Eucharist (communion), and singing spiritual songs. The gatherings were used primarily to celebrate the resurrection and to equip Christians to live as "salt and light" in their communities. Their methods of gathering were a direct expression of their purpose, and that purpose has not changed.

Today the church has veered from this common purpose, more intent on garnering the acceptance of outsiders than on being the church. The beauty of the church cannot be found in displaying Christianity as something inoffensively cool; this does a disservice to the Christian name by diluting the message of the gospel. The church does not need to be disseminators of relevance to be a credible voice in the public square.

The church, then, should also extend from a corporate expression to a personal way of life with regard to its purpose — individual believers living as extensions of Christ's unified body so that our mutual love and beautiful acts of service will glorify God. When the apostle Paul wrote the Ephesian church, he urged them to hold fast to Christ, to imitate him, living as children of light. Members of Christ's church should be growing into full maturity, becoming more and more like him, to *know* Christ. A healthy church is a church whose members are steeped in rich biblical learning, challenged in the spiritual disciplines and spurred on toward beautiful acts of service.[25] Eugene Peterson calls the church "the place and community where we are baptized into a Trinitarian identity," a gathering in which "we can be taught the Scriptures and learn to discern the ways that we follow Christ."[26] As we each live out this element of the church's purpose, we lead to the next main focus of church renewal — passion and devotion for God's Word.

In its infancy, Christianity spread because it demanded much from the convert, it was winsome, it cared for people, and it inspired martyrdom. These results stemmed from the church's deep sense of passion and devotion to God's Word. Church historian Michael Green notes, "Within thirty years of the founding of the new faith, to join the Christians meant to court martyrdom."[27] Yet the faith flourished. Through persecution, intimate community, and personal devotion to their faith, the infant church established a deeply rooted faith expression that would not be pulled up by any passing wind (trend) or threatening storm (heresy). It was a way of life that transcended culture because the Christians held fast to God's Word.

Perhaps we've veered from following closely to the Way because we find the pull of the culture too strong, and our rootedness in God's Word too weak. If so, then we need to return to our commitment to preach (those who are called to do so), study, and live out the Word of God regardless of what society deems acceptable. "The more at home the Word of God is among us," wrote German Reformer Philipp Jakob Spener, "the more we shall bring forth faith and its fruits."[28] This does not mean a muted and stagnant legalistic following of rules. Rather, it means a deep love of God's Word from which blossoms new life.

Here we look to our pastors and teachers and elders for guidance and a modeling that prizes solid biblical study, the public reading of Scripture during our "family gatherings," and its implementation in church discipline, the sacraments, and spiritual healing. This element of church renewal works like a hub from which we derive our purpose and with which we make disciples.

Disciple making is the beautiful process of sharing Christ with others through our lives — words and actions. It's interesting how in Jesus' leaving of his disciples, he left them, and us, the great Comforter. He told them that it was beneficial for him to leave so they could have the constant companionship of the Holy Spirit, who would always be there with them, in them.[29] The original word used by John, in his gospel account, is *paraklete*, which means "one called alongside of to help."[30] We can draw a lesson in discipleship from Jesus leaving us the Helper.

Just as we have an advocate, helper, comforter, and "truth revealer" in the Holy Spirit, likewise we should seek the same connection with one another in discipleship relationships with young Christians. True, discipleship takes time and, in large degree, is hard to quantify. It consists of building a trusting relationship that ebbs and flows over time – the teacher growing alongside of the disciple, encountering new aspects of life together, both conforming more and more to Christ.

———

Stripping our veneer is an inside-out idea. We first need the renewal that Paul wrote about: a transformation that takes place at the deepest recesses of the human heart with the aid of the Holy Spirit. Then, we need outward *exchanges.*

Exchanges serve as little beginning points designed to allow our spirits to stretch. They take aspects of the language of culture and replace them with the positive expressions found in the language of God. Exchanges are first steps to stripping our outer veneer and, given time, will become the natural by-product of our inner change. In pursuing Christ, we form a new perspective, a new way of being, and it's from this new perspective that we *do,* that we live.

"The great danger facing all of us," writes nineteenth-century pastor Philip Brooks, "is that some day we may wake up and find that we have been busy with the husks and trappings of life and have really missed life itself."[31] Exchanges help us slow down and *live*.

Exchange dissatisfaction for gratitude. You are blessed beyond belief. You have clean water, hospitals, and medicines. You have the opportunity for an education, to learn reading and writing and mathematics. You have access to affordable transportation. You have shelter, clothes, and food. Be thankful; all that you have needed his hand hath provided.[32]

Take one day a month and count your blessings. List all that you have, and then pray through the list, thanking God for his constant provision. Remember that none of it makes you who you are, and that, in fact, tomorrow everything you own could vanish. "Hold loosely to the things of this life," writes Holocaust survivor Corrie ten Boom. "That way if God requires them of you, it will be easy to let them go."

Thank God for meeting your physical needs, your health and full belly, your emotional needs, your friends and family and church. Take time to write a note of encouragement to those who have helped you along the way. You don't need to make the note long; anything that expresses your gratitude for their part in your life will bless them more than you realize.

Find thanks in your present and in your past. God has given you various circumstances that make you who you are; embrace them with gratitude. The good and the bad, the success and the failures are all part of God's loving guidance. As you learn to be thankful for your past, no matter what it is, you find deeper ways of sharing your life and giving hope to those around you.[33]

"Every time we decide to be grateful it will be easier to see new things to be grateful for," writes the late professor and author Henri Nouwen. "Gratitude begets gratitude, just as love begets love."[34]

Exchange getting for giving. In a society obsessed with accumulating as much as possible, what a refreshing idea to think of someone who constantly gives. Time, talents, money—whatever you can, give them generously. Make it a practice to keep an open hand; listen to God's promptings as you find new ways to lavish kindness on others. Hold your possessions loosely, "For we brought nothing into the world, and we can take nothing out of it."[35]

Giving acknowledges stewardship. We can be cheerful givers because we understand that everything we possess is God's. We're just managers.

Look for a reputable charity that connects with your heart and give them money. Start with a small donation if you like, but give something. Over time, increase the giving and the number of charities you support. Locally, look for families that may be in need of particular items such as coats for winter or a new air-conditioner or school supplies. Help them by donating these items to them. And if you can, do it anonymously.

Give more than your money; give of your time as well. Volunteer at a local charity, helping in ways that make sense with your natural talents and gifts. Or volunteer to help watch the kids so the neighbor can have more time to work on their project. Or better yet, get your hands dirty and help them finish the project.

Exchange hype for reality. Appreciate the small things in life that seem dull compared with the glitz and glamour of the hyper-real celebrity world. Enjoy a walk through your neighborhood. Take time to watch two squirrels zigzag through a tree, wrestling one another. Snuggle on the couch with your daughter and her favorite blanky. Celebrate the touchdown pass from you to your son in the backyard Super Bowl. Delight in the chance encounter at the store with an old friend.

Once a month, share a meal with your friends at each other's homes, trading hosting duties each time. Cook the meal as much from scratch as you can. Use vegetables grown in your garden and make your own bread and sauces and dressings. Appreciate the textures and colors and aromas of the food as you prepare the meal. Try not to let the preparation cause too much stress; instead, have fun with it. Use the time as a bit of mental relief, focusing only on the task at hand. In his book *My Bread,* Jim Lahey, baker and founder of the Sullivan Street Bakery in New York City, writes about his love affair with baking, "My mind is always in a bit of hyperactive turmoil, and the emotional escape bread baking brings, with its required focus and intensity, can push everything else away."[36]

If the meal doesn't turn out the way you wanted, don't worry about it. The pizza delivery person will appreciate the generous tip you leave as a thank-you for bailing you out of your cooking mishap. Ask your friends to leave their phones on the counter and to silence the ringer for the evening. Laugh and have fun together enjoying each other's company. Talk about the eternal things in life: your marriages, your kids, and your relationships. Keep your conversation uplifting and loving.

Exchange transaction for relation. When we chose to control and manipulate as the basis for our relationships, we skew our vision of others. We turn people to mere stepping-stones so we can "get things done." While these transactional interactions are effective, arguably, by the world's standards, this sort of skewed relationship hobbles true relationship and turns the other person into an object. We diminish our very humanity when we treat others this way, shattering the beauty of their individual purpose and meaning.[37]

Pastor and author Richard Foster reminds us that "human beings are infinitely precious beings because we are created in the image of God, but also because of the way we can enrich one another."[38] Stop looking at the people in your life as a one-sided relationship in which you leverage them for your gain.

Instead, take the focus off of yourself and place it on the other person. Put aside your needs and lift up the other's needs through your service to them. Let the love for your "neighbor" drive your decisions. Moving your selfish desires aside will strengthen relationships and give you confidence. And if fame or riches or success find you, point to the source of your success — Christ.

Spend time with someone whom you might otherwise ignore, someone who needs friendship or advice. Extend friendship to them, mentor them, help them grow; offer them your wisdom and counsel. Exchange your own enterprise with words and deeds that elevate others. Go out of your way to make them famous.

Exchange the common for the extraordinary. Bonhoeffer's definition of extraordinary reminds us that we are called to exemplify the uncommon in our lives, to act in ways that stand in stark contrast to the ways of society. You are a resident here, and naturally you will be a participant, but what does your behavior look like?

In your marriage, be disciplined, maintain self-control, and model an unselfish love. Don't speak harshly of your spouse in public. Cherish them and remember that your marriage models Christ's love for the church.

In your work, don't view business as a means to profit. Look for ways to do more with your profession than just make money. Don't get trapped in company politics. Avoid brown-nosing and unfair negotiations and water-cooler gossip.[39]

"But what happens when we live God's way? He brings gifts into our lives, much the same way that fruit appears in an orchard — things like affection for others, exuberance about life, serenity. We develop a willingness to stick with things, a sense of compassion in the heart, and a conviction that a basic holiness permeates things and people. We find ourselves involved in loyal commitments, not needing to force our way in life, able to marshal and direct our energies wisely ... Among those who belong to Christ, everything connected with getting our own way and mindlessly responding to what everyone else calls necessities is killed off for good — crucified."[40]

—

An ancient document exists from the second or third century that reveals the early Christians' character. It's referred to as "The So-Called Letter to Diognetus." The letter presents Christians as "The New Race" or "The Third Race"—a distinct people within Greco-Roman society.[41] The Christians described in this letter expressed their faith through action, but only as a by-product of pursuing Jesus.

They didn't live as eccentrics, and there was nothing out of the ordinary concerning their "country or language or customs."[42] They didn't move from their villages and cities to form a commune, nor did elite philosophers or leaders form their teaching. But even though they looked and acted like other citizens, their core beliefs, devotion to Jesus, and way of life set them apart.

They contributed to society but didn't pursue their own desires. They set a higher moral standard than what was required of them by the state. This heavenly standard also translated into loving interaction with one another and the world. Yet even with these high standards, people still found reasons to persecute them.

One section of the letter in particular displays just how unveneered these Christians lived. It reads, "They are unknown, and still they are condemned; they are put to death, and yet they are brought to life.... They are completely destitute, and yet they enjoy complete abundance. They are dishonored, and in their very dishonor are glorified."[43] This letter reveals the great paradox of the Christian faith: followers of Christ living side by side with the rest of the world, yet untouched by the language of culture. Their manner of living serves as a lovely reminder to us that the Christian life should be lived unto Jesus, in humble service.

Those who choose Christ look to his life and death and "put him on," as Paul says, living in a way that triumphs in death, empties itself to be filled, and loses itself to be found. Look at the words *unknown, destitute*, and *dishonored* from the quote. Who in today's world would find these words to be valuable life modifiers? Not many.

But for the Christian, life is a constant stripping, just as it was for Jesus. The idea of the incarnation, Jesus' emptying himself, baffles us. God, shrouded in glory, condescends to humanity and sends us his unique Son. Jesus, the very *Logos* of the universe, becomes a man and lives among us. Paul says that he took on the very nature of a bondservant. He dove into humanity, and then went even farther and descended into death itself to bring forth life — not just any life but an eternal one. "Death and rebirth — go down to go up — it is a key principle," writes C. S. Lewis in his book *Miracles*. "Through this bottleneck, this belittlement, the highroad nearly always lies."[44] Jesus belittled himself and reached into death, through the splintered brutality of the cross, and emerged as a piece of weathered barn siding does after the reclaiming process: his scars bringing life, his beatings renewing all things, an atoning patina for humankind.

The renewing effect of Jesus' emptying and resurrection carries over into his followers. These final lines encapsulate the beauty of Diognetus' letter best: "It is true that they are 'in the flesh,' but they do not live 'according to the flesh.' They busy themselves on earth, but their citizenship is in heaven.... They love all men, and by all men are persecuted.... They are poor, and yet they make many rich.... They are reviled, and yet they bless.... To put it simply: What the soul is in the body, that Christians are in the world."[45] What an arresting thought; we almost get the sense that these early Christians lived with their "hearts burning"[46] within them at all times.

But what of us? When the world encounters the Christian presence in their neighborhoods, governments, and schools, does our rhetoric make them want to breathe deeply the beautiful life before them? Do they discover that even as they belittle the Christian's faith, the Christian seems only to rise? Do they wonder how the Christian can seem to be totally engaged in this world but completely unaffected by it? Perhaps, as we work toward the unveneered life, all Christians should adopt this statement as their filter: am I being the soul of the world?

BACK AT THE SAWMILL

The Language of Restoration

Behold, I make all things new.

— *Jesus of Nazareth*

Our husbands cheat on us. Our wives stop talking to us. We lose our jobs. We make mistakes, lots of them. We screw up. We let our friends down, and they let us down. This is the muck of life. But we are all knee deep in it and faced with a choice: do we give in to a world content with living with a veneer, or do we choose a new life, the unveneered life?

To live this life, we must find a way to strip our veneer and discover a renewed existence, one unbound by the trappings of the world. So when life exposes us at our weakest moments, we're at peace knowing that God sees us through the holy prism of his Son, allowing us to stand before him reverent yet expectant, humble yet confident.

The trials of life should not cause us to veneer. Instead, they ought to free us. We should stand unashamed before the world, bruised and battered, yet moving from glory to glory. Remember, the beauty from the antique wood comes from the patina, the character produced through its life.

Through the eternal lens of redemption, our scars become part of the beauty, part of what makes us unique.

The unveneered life unfolds its rich beauty as it extends through the years. Time allows healing and repentance and openness. Our scars heal as beauty marks.

As redeemed humans, we rest in the confidence of God's eternal love. We're not lost to ourselves but rather are at home in the family of God. We find his love wraps us closer than any veneer could and "keeps the cold out better than a cloak."[1] Suddenly we begin finding pieces of the eternal in our relationships. We begin to break down the barriers of isolation and loneliness. We experience life together, truly.

———

Back at the old sawmill, as the sun yawns across the Pennsylvania horizon, the autumn air whistles through the sparse pines at the back of the lot. Dean checks in with his foreman. They chat about clients and orders and their new load of hickory that just arrived. They lock up together and wave off the day; Dean lingers just a few moments as his friend drives off toward home.

After he fastens the bottom three buttons of his flannel jacket, Dean reaches into the chest pocket for a lighter and a cigar—a reward for a long day. He tucks his head into his coat to catch the flame, protecting the fire from the sweeping breeze.

As he looks up, the sunset grabs his breath. The colors of the day slip into twilight and stop him for a moment. He catches a glimpse of the relentless cycle—morning and evening, then morning again. The sun dips behind the western treeline. He exhales. He's thought about it before, tonight isn't the first time: the repetition of it all, the day-in, day-out of what he does. How his work never seems to change. How it can start to consume him and keep him from the things that matter.

He thinks about his life with God. The mysterious journey that put him here, right here, in the middle of a sawmill on a Thursday night in early autumn. Fifteen years ago, Dean might have been heading to a party. But tonight, he can't wait to get home. Maybe he'll stop by and surprise the grandkids and read them a book before bed.

Strange, but in the repetition, Dean finds an eerie peace. Who would have guessed that a guy like Dean could turn out okay? But he did. God renewed Dean's life, reclaiming what most would see as wasted time.

Turning off the lights, Dean steps over a pile of lumber waiting for a turn in the kiln. In a couple of weeks, this batch will be finished with the reclaiming process and make its way to a new house somewhere east of the Blue Ridge. An old barn, dilapidated and battered, reclaimed, and now beautiful flooring.

Even after the intense restoration, the wood won't be perfect. But it will have purpose now, a reason to be. No longer rotting away in a field, it collects the markings of a young family growing, failing, and celebrating their way through life.

Like the wood, and like Dean, we're all going through a restoration process: the process of healing, the process of finding beauty, and the process of discovering purpose. The nails of life are pulled from our grain; our blackened surface, that was pounded by shame, is now smoothed. Purpose found, we wait to offer hope to someone in need of true beauty, the beauty of the imperfect.

AUTHORS' NOTE

NO TEARS IN THE WRITER, NO TEARS IN THE READER.

NO SURPRISE IN THE WRITER, NO SURPRISE IN THE READER.

— Robert Frost

In the past, Randall's Island served as a home for orphans, juvenile delinquents, and the poor. Located in New York City's East River, the island is now an expanse of green that functions as a sports complex and concert venue. And in September of 1996, the island played host to Seattle grunge band Pearl Jam, who were on tour supporting their latest album, *No Code*.

That September, my brother and I (Jason) made the beautiful fall drive from Virginia to northeastern Pennsylvania. From there we picked up my future wife and her brother, and some other friends, and then headed into New York for the Randall's Island show. Tim (my coauthor), who lived in Pennsylvania at the time, also drove up for the show with one of his brothers and some friends.

When Tim and I met for the first time in 2004, we started listing our favorite songs and bands and concerts we had attended. It took about two minutes for us to figure out we both were Pearl Jam fans and both had attended the Randall's Island show in the fall of 1996. Reminiscing about the show, we realized we probably had sat no more than ten yards away from each other.

Over the course of the next several years, we became fast friends and our conversation moved from music to culture to church. It was a natural conversational progression since I work in the world of design and branding, and Tim worked in the church world. My work at the studio kept me busy making clients look "good," while Tim worked as a freelance writer, producing curriculum for church leaders.

As we talked, we started to wonder why everything in society seemed so backward. Enron was still in the news for false accounting practices that inflated the value of their stocks. Bernie Madoff was making headlines for bilking investors of millions. McMansions purchased with no-interest loans peppered the suburban landscape. Credit card offers filled mailboxes, making it easy to buy anything you could want with no payments for ninety days.

All the while, the well-documented rise of the "consumer church" was taking place. The relevance movement was in full swing as churches clamored to look hip and adopt the latest trends to get more people through the doors. Our late-night discussions with friends at the pub seemed to revolve around the serious flaws we saw in the world. As Christians, Tim and I couldn't escape the reality that society seemed to be influencing the church instead of the church influencing society.

The original notes for the book are nothing more than a handful of thoughts that read like an angst-filled, distorted-guitar, grunge-rock middle-finger "we're not gonna take it" anthem that we scratched out in our Moleskine notebooks. But over time, our immediate reaction evolved to more of a thoughtful interaction on the topic.

As we debated ideas, sought counsel, and read, we discovered that these societal issues were by-products of our human condition. And we couldn't separate our Christian faith from the solution; our view of God shaped the entire discussion. Our response became less about our anger toward the world, Christians, and the church, and more about our wanting something different for the world, Christians, and the church.

So the idea for *Veneer* was born. Throughout the book project, both of us had to examine our lives and our expressions and our interactions with society. It's easy to look at society and critique it, to point at other people and offer solutions to their problems. But what about us? What about Tim? What about Jason? How were we buying into the lies of the world? How were we contributing to the consumer church?

Along the way, many conversations were sparked with friends and family as Tim and I each dealt with the effects society was having on our lives. We had to wrestle with our insecurities and shortcomings and hang-ups. We also had to wrestle with God, confessing our own lack of faith, straining toward a more intimate relationship with him, and understanding what it means to follow him in this world. If this book is written to anyone, it's written to us.

Back at the Pearl Jam show in 1996, lead singer Eddie Vedder broke into a speech during "Porch," the last song of the night. "I hope you know who you are," he proclaimed. "If you don't know who you are, figure it out, cause you are somebody."[1]

That is our hope for this book: that it will help you figure out who you are. That it will help you figure out how you are meant to live. That the world will make a little more sense to you. And that you will make a little more sense to the world. Vedder is right; you are somebody.

ACKNOWLEDGMENTS

I'M A LUCKY MAN TO COUNT
ON BOTH HANDS THE ONES I LOVE.

– Eddie Vedder

A couple of years after Jason and I met, he invited me to a small Thursday morning gathering at the Southern breakfast staple, the Waffle House. Jason had spent the last five years meeting his pastor, Jon Adams, and two others for eggs, hash browns, bacon, and what Southerners refer to as coffee. Northerners might call it engine cleaner. Two of the regulars dropped out of the group, so they needed a replacement. I obliged.

Over the next three years, we added other people to the group, and together the four, sometimes five, of us read through books, argued over the definition of modern-day evangelism, and developed an immunity to engine cleaner. Our small Thursday gathering has become a safe haven for our ideas, anxieties, and struggles. It's a place where we collaborate, not for work, necessarily, but for our lives.

The idea and writing of *Veneer* emerged from such an environment; from Waffle House mornings, to the North Georgia and North Carolina mountains, to Pennsylvania bonfires, to Athens work days, to the Pub, to Sunday evenings sitting on the back porch, this book has been influenced by the minds and hearts of our beloved friends and family. Jason and I are indebted to the push and pull of these lives collaborating with ours.

To the thought shapers—thank you: Gabe Lyons, Jon Adams, Brent Cole, Ben Ortlip, Christine Willard, Heather Locy, Søren Kierkegaard, Eddie Veddar, Dr. David Wells, Bach ("Suite for Cello in D Major"), Jesus son of Mary and Unique Son of God, St. Bernardus, the Paraklete, YHWH, Bonne Maman.

To our friends who graciously plodded through our first drafts, sent encouraging emails, and lovingly critiqued our ideas—thank you: Dave Blanchard, Jennifer Ask, Byron Borger, Scott Kauffmann, Brian Miller, Beth Nelson, Josh Locy, Kerry Priest, Johnny Carr, Dr. Alan Myatt, Sajan George, Chris and Monica Van Allsburg, Jordan Vance, Khloe Keener, Alyssa Weaver, Rebekah Sauder.

To those who kick-started the project and believed in it from the beginning: Brad Lomenick, Ken Coleman, Scott Calgaro, Margaret Feinberg, Jon Merritt.

To the teams at Yates and Yates and Zondervan who

have worked tirelessly to move this book forward — thank you: Christopher Ferebee, Matt Yates, Curtis Yates, Sealy Yates, Angela Scheff, Don Gates, Mike Salisbury, Brian Phipps, Curt Diepenhorst, Joyce Ondersma.

I (Tim) would like to extend a special thanks to my wife, Christine: for your patience and long-suffering throughout the duration of this project, for quiet discussions by the fire about our dreams, and for seeing past my veneer and loving me anyway. To my little girls, Lyric and Brielle: you don't realize now what you meant to me through this writing process, but I promise you, the laughter and delight you bring to my life is priceless; I am more of a man only because you help me grow more childlike in my faith. To my family: Mom and Dad, Renee and Mike, Jon and Kathy, Robin and Jeff, Michael and Katlin — your love and encouragement continue to water my soul. I see a picture of being unveneered because I see each of you growing toward heaven. I love you all. To the Fire Family: I think we touched the night sky. To Gabe Lyons: for believing first. I owe you a tennis match. To Brent Cole: For morning discussions at the Grit, debates at the Trapeze, and for "cut throat busted sunsets." To Steve Beecham: you provided "The Swig," our secluded haven from which to write. To Jason Locy: there's a trapdoor in the sun, my friend.

I (Jason) would like to extend a special thanks to Tim

Willard, a great collaborator and friend. Gabe Lyons for a lifelong friendship and for the countless words of encouragement. This book wouldn't have happened if it were not for your support. To Brent Cole, the tireless sounding board. Patricio Juarez and the rest of the FiveStone gang for always making me look good. My brother Josh, for challenging my thoughts and splitting the costs of Christmas time visits to Pops. Mom and Dad for encouraging me and believing in me. I have only recently realized how much I was shaped by your positive contributions to my life. I appreciate you guys. Ethan, Christian, and Naomi – thanks for your patience as I worked on the book. Sorry that "the book isn't very long." Heather, thank-you for all that you did while I worked on the book. Your patience with the process should earn you the biggest crown the angels make. Thank you for graciously and honestly pointing out the veneer in my life; I am a better person because of you.

NOTES

Prelude

1. From Eric Carle's classic, *The Very Hungry Caterpillar*.

Chapter 1: Sawmill

1. This is a paraphrase of lyrics from Randy Travis's "Forever and Ever, Amen."
2. "Tom Ford: From Fashion to Film with 'A Single Man,'" interview by Terry Gross, *Fresh Air*, NPR, December 14, 2009, *http://www.npr.org/templates/transcript/transcript .php?storyId=121405891*.
3. Peter Kreeft, *Back to Virtue: Traditional Moral Wisdom for Modern Moral Confusion* (San Francisco: Ignatius, 1992), 37.
4. Brennan Manning, *The Importance of Being Foolish* (San Francisco: HarperOne, 2005), 127.
5. Eugene Peterson, *The Jesus Way* (Grand Rapids, Mich.: Eerdmans, 2007), 8. We were delighted to find that the introduction to this book deals with veneer concepts. Peterson is a shepherd-pastor who has a deep understanding of what we are up against in our culture.

Chapter 2: Celebrity Me

1. In his book *The Image*, Daniel Boorstin develops the popular definition of a celebrity, "A person known for [their] well-knowness" (Daniel J. Boorstin, *The Image: A Guide to Pseudo-Events in America* [New York: Vintage, 1992], 57). Neal Gabler later amended that definition by stating, "Celebrities were self-contained entertainment, a form of entertainment that was rapidly exceeding film and television in popularity" (Neal Gabler, *Life: The Movie: How Entertainment Conquered Reality* [New York: Vintage, 1998], 146). Our definition is a synthesis of both ideas.
2. Quoted in Gabler, *Life: The Movie*, 148–49.
3. Chris Hedges, *Empire of Illusion* (New York: Nation, 2009), 29.
4. Lynn Hirschberg, "The Self-Manufacture of Megan Fox," *New York Times Magazine*, November 11, 2009, *http://www.nytimes.com/2009/11/15/magazine/15Fox-t.html*.
5. Jason Tanz, "Internet Famous: Julia Allison and the Secrets of Self-Promotion," *Wired*, August 2008, *http://www.wired.com/culture/lifestyle/magazine/16 – 08/howto_allison*.
6. William Deresiewicz writes, "The camera has created a culture of celebrity ... the computer is creating a culture of connectivity ... Celebrity and connectivity are both ways of becoming known. This is what the contemporary self wants. It wants to be recognized, wants to be connected: It wants to be visible. If not to the millions, on *Survivor* or *Oprah*, then to the hundreds, on Twitter or Facebook" (William Deresiewicz, "The End of Solitude," *Chronicle of Higher Education* 55, no. 21 [January 30, 2009]: B6, quoted in Hedges, *Empire of Illusion*, 22).

7. Sherry Turkle, *Life on the Screen* (New York: Simon and Schuster, 1997), 26.

8. Luke 4:1–13.

9. In *The Grand Inquisitor* by Fyodor Dostoyevsky, the devil is referred to as "the dread and intelligent spirit."

10. Matt. 4:4 NIV.

11. Mark 9:35 NIV.

12. John 6:38. Jesus also prays for his Father's will in the garden just before he was betrayed. See Luke 22:42.

13. Klaus Bockmuehl, *The Christian Way of Living* (Vancouver: Regent College Publishing, 1998), 35.

14. Henri Nouwen, *In the Name of Jesus* (New York: Crossroad, 2000), 63.

15. James 1:27.

16. C. S. Lewis, *The Screwtape Letters* (Uhrichsville, Ohio: Barbour, 1990), 45–46.

17. These notes on the specific idols of influence, approval, and achievement were taken from "The Luther Project," a private study given by Timothy Keller.

18. Ralph C. Wood, *Contending for the Faith: The Church's Engagement with Culture* (Waco: Baylor Univ. Press, 2003), 169.

19. Craig Gay, *The Way of the Modern World: Or, Why It's Tempting to Live as if God Doesn't Exist* (Grand Rapids, Mich.: Eerdmans, 1998), 196.

20. Bockmuehl, *The Christian Way of Living*, 57.

21. Dietrich Bonhoeffer, *The Cost of Discipleship* (New York: Touchstone, 1995), 152.

22. Ibid., 146. In his discussion, Bonhoeffer references Matt. 5:43–48. Matt. 5:47 contains the word *perissos*.

23. Ibid., 157.

Chapter 3: The Queen Is Dead – Long Live the Queen

1. Christopher Hibbert, *Elizabeth I: A Personal History of the Virgin Queen* (New York: Penguin, 2001), 73.

2. Mark Gottdiener, *New Forms of Consumption: Consumers, Culture, and Commodification* (Lanham, Md.: Rowman and Littlefield, 2000), 12.

3. Grant McCracken, *Culture and Consumerism* (Bloomington: Indiana Univ. Press, 1990), 11, 15.

4. Ibid., 11.

5. Ibid., 9. It should be noted that although Queen Elizabeth is not credited with the advent of consumerism, she did introduce a mindset of consumeristic manipulation. Grant McCracken cites Chandra Mukerji as pinpointing the rise of the "consumerist culture" in fifteenth- and sixteenth-century Europe. "She examines the emergence of early modern printing, eighteenth-century cotton, and the development of three aspects of materialism."

6. Ibid., 16–20.

7. Ibid.

8. David Lyon, *Postmodernity* (Minneapolis: Univ. of Minnesota, 1999), 21.

9. Daniel Boorstin, *The Image* (New York: Vintage, 1992), 215.

10. This number was reported in 2008 by Jay Walker-Smith, president of Yankelovich, a consumer behavior research firm. Our guess is this number has increased a bit.

11. This number represents the revenue generated from the 883 reporting agencies as reported by *Advertising Age*: *http://adage.com/agencynews/article?article_id=143467*.

12. Grant McCracken, *Culture and Consumerism II: Markets, Meaning, and Brand Management* (Bloomington: Indiana Univ. Press, 2005), 181.

13. Scott Bedbury, *A New Brand World* (New York: Penguin, 2003), 14.

14. Ibid.

15. Bedbury makes the point that the needs are part of Maslow's hierarchy.

16. Anthony K. Hoekema, *Created in the Image of God* (Grand Rapids, Mich.: Eerdmans, 1986), 216. Hoekema references 1 Cor. 15:12–57 and Rom. 8:23 as primary passages that point to the body and soul as a "psychosomatic unity" (203–18). See also Robert H. Gundry, *Soma in Biblical Theology* (Grand Rapids, Mich.: Zondervan, 1987), 201. Gundry puts it like this: "Substantively, man is a duality – i.e., a proper unity of two parts – of spirit and body."

17. Col. 2:8–10.

18. Col. 2:8, *http://biblestudy.crosswalk.com/mybst/default.aspx?type=bible&translation=KJV&bookcode =col&bookname=Colossians&chapterid=2&verseid=8*, 2008, *http://www.crosswalk.com/* (accessed November 2008). In context, Paul is warning against subversive teaching from Judaic-oriental heretics who taught philosophies that later led to Gnosticism. These philosophies were popular in the culture, as Colossae was known to have a magical and mystical cultural bent.

19. Edward Farley, *Ecclesial Reflection* (Philadelphia: Fortress, 1982), 232, quoted in Alistair McFadyen, *The Call to Personhood* (Cambridge: Cambridge Univ. Press, 1990), 236.

20. In his book *Spent*, Geoffrey Miller states that "consumerism actually promotes two big lies." One lie Miller points out is that consumerism used to enhance traits such as "physical appearance, apparent intelligence, personality, or moral virtues" may work to fool people in the short term, but no one will be fooled in the long term. Geoffrey Miller, *Spent: Sex, Evolution, and Consumer Behavior* (New York: Penguin, 2009), 84.

21. McFadyen, *The Call to Personhood*, 45.

22. Phil. 3:8 NLT.

Chapter 1: The Great Vanishing

1. Hannah Arendt, *The Human Condition* (Chicago: Univ. of Chicago Press, 1998), 134.

2. Facebook statistics and background were taken from Lev Grossman, "2010 Person of the Year Mark Zuckerberg," *Time*, double issue, December 21, 2010 and January 3, 2011, 46.

3. Jaron Lanier, *You Are Not a Gadget: A Manifesto* (New York: Knopf, 2010), 4.

4. Penelope Green, "Yours for the Peeping," *New York Times*, November 4, 2007, *http://www.nytimes.com/2007/11/04/weekinreview/04green.html?pagewanted=1&_r=1&sq =sherry%20turkle&st=cse&scp=6*.

5. G. W. Leibniz, *Discourse on Metaphysics*, trans. Daniel Garber and Roger Ariew (Cambridge: Hackett, 1991), 39.

6. There are eight rules to Fight Club:
1. The first rule to Fight Club is, you do not talk about Fight Club.
2. The second rule to Fight Club is, you *do not* talk about Fight Club.
3. If someone says stop, goes limp, taps out, the fight is over.
4. Two guys to a fight.
5. One fight at a time.
6. No shirts, no shoes.
7. Fights will go on as long as they have to.
8. If this is your first night at Fight Club, you have to fight.

Chapter 5: Oh, Inverted World

* Apologies to the Shins for using the title of their first album as the title for this chapter.
1. Alan Schroeder, *Presidential Debates: Fifty Years of High-Risk TV* (New York: Columbia Univ. Press, 2008), 2–7.
2. Quoted in David Gergen, *Eyewitness to Power: The Essence of Leadership, Nixon to Clinton* (New York: Simon and Schuster, 2000), 84.
3. Michael Dobbs, "The Fact Checker," *Washington Post*, September 26, 2008, 9:33 p.m., *http://voices.washingtonpost.com/fact-checker/2008/09/debate_live_fact_check_starts.html*.
4. The lowering of testing standards is a well-documented problem. The situation presented here is a direct representation of a *New York Times* article from October 29, 2009. Since then, the Obama administration has worked to overhaul the program, calling on states to raise academic standards. See Sam Dillon, "Federal Researchers Find Lower Standards in Schools," *New York Times*, October 29, 2009, *http://www.nytimes.com/2009/10/30/education/30educ.html?_r=3&emc=*.
5. The examples of obsolesence in the auto industry used here are taken from chapter 2 of Giles Slade, *Made to Break: Technology and Obsolescence in America* (Cambridge: Harvard Univ. Press, 2006), 29.
6. See Gen. 11:1–9.
7. Thomas Merton, *The New Man* (New York: Farrar, Strauss, and Giroux, 1961), 59, 50.
8. "Police: As Many as 20 Present at Gang Rape outside School Dance," *CNN.com*, October 27, 2009, *http://articles.cnn.com/2009-10-27/justice/California.gang.rape.investigation_1_suspects-arrest-police?_s=pm:crime*.
9. David Bazan (Pedro the Lion), "Penetration."
10. Jacques Ellul, *Propaganda: The Formation of Men's Attitudes* (New York: Knopf, 1965), 8.
11. Helmut Thielicke, *Our Heavenly Father: Sermons on the Lord's Prayer* (New York: Harper and Brothers, 1960), 57.
12. There is a difference between elevating the self over God—individualism—and celebrating our individuality. Individualism, by definition, stresses self-reliance, whereas individuality describes personal quality of character, differentiating one person from another.
13. As an aside, we must say that we offer these observations for what they are: a clear and honest look at an honorable position in the body of Christ. We (Jason and Tim) meet with our pastor every Thursday at Waffle House. We love our pastor. Tim's

NOTES

father has been a pastor his whole life. Both of these men have heard these observations and in large part agree with what has happened to the pastorate in the twenty-first-century church. We offer these observations in a spirit of love.

14. Michael Horton, "All Crossed Up," *Touchstone*, March 2008, *http://www.touchstonemag.com /archives/article.php?id=21 – 02 – 011-v.*

15. 1 Peter 5:1 – 4.

16. John Piper, *Brothers We Are Not Professionals: A Plea to Pastors for Radical Ministry* (Nashville: B&H Publishing, 2002), 84 – 85.

17. F. F. Bruce, *Paul: Apostle of the Heart Set Free* (Grand Rapids, Mich.: Eerdmans, 1977), 249.

18. David B. Capes, Rodney Reeves, and E. Randolph Richards, *Rediscovering Paul: An Introduction to His World, Letters and Theology* (Downers Grove, Ill.: InterVarsity, 2007), 144.

19. Bruce W. Winter, *After Paul Left Corinth: The Influence of Secular Ethics and Social Change* (Grand Rapids, Mich.: Eerdmans, 2001), 203.

20. Francis Chan, "Beyond the Trend," *Catalyst Groupzine* 5, 2009.

21. Eugene Peterson, *The Jesus Way* (Grand Rapids, Mich.: Eerdmans, 2007), 1.

22. Quoted in Luisa Kroll, "Megachurches, Megabusiness," *Forbes*, September 17, 2003, *http://forbes.com/2003/09/17/cz_lk_0917megachurch.html.*

23. Peterson, *The Jesus Way*, 1.

Interlude

1. Sea Wolf, "The Garden You Planted."

2. Throughout the remainder the book, we will be using the word *transcendent*. To be clear as to what we mean, we are using the word the way D. A. Carson defines it in his book *The Gagging of God*: "God exists apart from the creation he made, and thus above space and time. Thus he is not in any way dependent upon his creation; he is self-existing – that is, he draws his own existence only from himself. He is absolute." D. A. Carson, *The Gagging of God* (Grand Rapids, Mich.: Zondervan, 1996), 223.

   We also refer to God as "other," which is simply another way to say he is transcendent –
   that he is above space and time. Christ spoke of his transcendence when he said, "I am not of this world" (John 8:23). Again in John 8:58 he said "*ego eimi*" or "I exist." Jesus here uses a double emphatic. He was and is and is to come.

3. Alistair McFadyen, *The Call to Personhood* (Cambridge: Cambridge Univ. Press, 1990), 61.

4. Ibid., 61.

5. 2 Cor. 4:8 – 10, 16 – 18 NASB.

Chapter 6: Whale Stars

1. God is immutable. He never changes. But in the veneer world, we try to box him in, control him like the rest of our lives, and in that, we set expectations for him.

2. Oswald Chambers, *My Utmost for His Highest* (Uhrichsville, Ohio: Barbour, 1963), 118.

3. 2 Tim. 3:1 – 2 ESV.

4. Gertrude Himmelfarb, *The De-Moralization of Society: From Victorian Virtues to Modern Values* (New York: Knopf, 1994), 11.

5. Matt. 22:37–39 ESV.

6. John Stott, *The Cross of Christ* (Downers Grove, Ill.: InterVarsity, 2006), 269.

7. Eph. 4:20–24 ESV.

8. Rom. 12:3 ESV.

9. Matt. 16:24 ESV.

10. Stott, *The Cross of Christ*, 269.

11. Chambers, *My Utmost for His Highest*, 118.

12. T. S. Eliot, "Choruses from the Rock," 1934.

13. *Experience* as defined in *The American Heritage Dictionary*: "*n.* The apprehension of an object, thought, or emotion through the sense or mind. Active participation in events or activities, leading to the accumulation of knowledge. *v.* To participate in personally." Even by definition, we find the idea of experiencing God to be self-focused.

14. Eugene Peterson, *The Jesus Way* (Grand Rapids, Mich.: Eerdmans, 2007), 110.

15. Ps. 50:3 NIV.

16. Eph. 4:6 NIV.

17. John 14:26 NIV.

18. Alistair McFadyen, *The Call to Personhood* (Cambridge: Cambridge Univ. Press, 1990), 113–26.

19. Eccl. 5:2.

20. Richard Foster, *Prayer: Finding the Heart's True Home* (San Francisco: HarperOne, 1992), 65.

21. A. W. Tozer, *The Pursuit of God* (Camp Hill, Pa.: Christian Publications, 1993), 86.

22. Quoted in Richard Foster, *The Freedom of Simplicity* (San Francisco: HarperOne, 1981), 78.

Chapter 7: *The Violence of Bees*

1. With other religions, life precedes love, meaning that there was no love prior to life. And if there was no love before life, then those religions are based on a mono god, a god who is in its essence merely one, singular. Not so with the God of the Bible.

2. Col. 1:15–16 (ESV) says, "For by him all things were created, in heaven and on earth, visible and invisible, whether thrones or dominions or rulers or authorities—all things were created through him and for him."

3. Cornelius Plantinga Jr., *Engaging God's World: A Christian Vision of Faith, Learning, and Living* (Grand Rapids, Mich.: Eerdmans, 2002), 23.

4. John 14:15–17.

5. John 16:14.

6. *The American Heritage Dictionary*.

7. Tim's brother-in-law, Mike, said this to him once. It always evoked tears from Mike. Reflecting on the idea that God's love is so fierce that he would send his Son is jarring.

8. John 3:16. Our Bible translations could do a little better with the phrase "only begotten" or "one and only" Son. A more faithful rendering would be God's "unique" or "one-of-a-kind" Son. It is the word *monogenesis*, and it carries distinction. See Andreas J.

Kostenberger and Scott R. Swain, *Father, Son, and Spirit: The Trinity and John's Gospel* (Downers Grove, Ill.: InterVarsity, 2008), 75–92, for an in-depth explanation.

9. St. Augustine, *Confessions* (Oxford: Oxford Univ. Press, 1998), 273.

10. Titus 3:5 NET, emphasis added.

11. Isa. 38:17 NET.

12. Augustine, *Confessions*, 273.

13. In his lectures, Dr. Tim Laniak, academic dean at Gordon-Conwell Charlotte campus, gives a beautiful explanation of how God weaves the family motif throughout the entire Bible. His lectures added depth to this understanding for us.

14. Andreas Kostenberger and Scott Swain, in their lively discussion on the Trinity, write, "God is shown to take the initiative not only in creation but also in redemptive history.... Believers are said to be 'born from God'" (Kostenberger and Swain, *Father, Son, and Spirit*, 50). For anyone interested in a thorough treatment of the Trinity in the fourth gospel, this is the book.

15. Gal. 4:5 NLT.

16. Rom. 8:15, 23 NLT.

17. J. I. Packer, *Knowing God* (Downers Grove, Ill.: InterVarsity, 1973), 211.

18. 2 Cor. 13:14 KJV.

19. John Fawcett, "Blest Be the Tie That Binds."

Chapter 8: Transcend

1. Phileena Heuertz, *Pilgrimage of a Soul: Contemplative Spirituality for the Active Life* (Downers Grove, Ill.: InterVarsity, 2010), 149.

2. Prov. 27:6.

3. James Joyce, *A Portrait of the Artist as a Young Man* (New York: Bantam, 1992), 147–58.

4. John 13:3–4 ESV.

5. Phil. 2:5–8.

6. Eph. 5:2 ESV, emphases added.

7. Craig Gay, *The Way of the Modern World* (Grand Rapids, Mich.: Eerdmans, 1998), 294.

8. 1 Cor. 13:4–6.

9. Klaus Bockmuehl, *The Christian Way of Living* (Vancouver: Regent College Publishing, 1994), 45.

10. Frederick Buechner, *The Magnificent Defeat* (New York: HarperCollins, 1966), 105.

11. Phil. 2:1–4.

12. Song 8:6–7.

13. Taken from Ray LaMontagne's "Empty."

14. Ibid.

15. Jonathan Edwards, *A Treatise Concerning Religious Affections* (Dublin: George Caw Printer, 1812), 9.

16. The term *strong force* was used by Kenneth Boa in a private lecture.

17. Rom. 8:34–35 NIV.

18. Rom. 8:35–37 NIV.

19. Søren Kierkegaard, *Works of Love* (New York: HarperPerennial, 2009), 247.

Chapter 9: Vapor Sunshine

1. Philip Gibbs, *Now It Can Be Told* (New York: Harper and Brothers, 1920), 131.
2. Ernest Hemingway, *The Sun Also Rises* (New York: Scribner, 1926), 17.
3. Ibid., introductory pages.
4. Ps. 144:4.
5. T. S. Eliot, "The Hollow Men," *Complete Poems and Plays: 1909 – 1950* (New York: Harcourt and Brace, 1952), 56.
6. D. A. Carson et al., eds., *New Bible Commentary: 21st Century Edition*, Accordance electronic edition (Downers Grove, Ill.: InterVarsity, 1994), 608.
7. Eccl. 2:24 – 25 NLT, emphases added.
8. Eccl. 12:13 NLT.
9. Eliot, "The Hollow Men," *Complete Poems and Plays*, 57.
10. Ibid., 59.
11. A nonchronological expression of the following Scriptures: Ps. 51:2 – 14; Jonah 2:6 NET; Lam. 3:19 – 21; Rev. 22:16 – 17 NET; John 8:12 NLT; Matt. 11:28 – 30; Isa. 40:31.
12. Eccl. 3:11 NLT.
13. C. S. Lewis, *Surprised by Joy* (New York: Harvest, 1955), 179.
14. Interview of Jack Murray on StoryCorps, *http://storycorps.org/listen/stories/jack-murray.*
15. "Church Attendance Back to Normal," *FoxNews.com*, September 11, 2002, *http://www.foxnews.com/story/0,2933,62674,00.html.*
16. John 15:1, 4 NASB.
17. Søren Kierkegaard, *Works of Love* (New York: HarperPerennial, 2009), 281 – 82.
18. John 15:10 – 12 NET.
19. John 15:13 – 15.
20. Craig S. Keener, *The IVP Bible Background Commentary: New Testament* (Downers Grove, Ill.: InterVarsity, 1993), 301.
21. Ibid.
22. Gay, *The Way of the Modern World*, 216.
23. Matt. 6:31 – 32.
24. Matt. 6:33 ESV.
25. Matt. 6:34.

Chapter 10: End Veneer

1. Ps. 131:3 TNIV.
2. The full account of David dancing in the street and the following encounter can be read in 2 Samuel 6.
3. Ps. 139:3, 13 – 14 ESV.
4. Acts 13:22 ESV.
5. To read the full account, see 1 Chronicles 15 NLT.
6. This idea is crystallized in Chuck Swindoll's book *David: A Man of Passion and Destiny* (Nashville: Thomas Nelson, 1997), 144.

NOTES

7. Read the full account of Nathan's confronting David with a parable regarding his affair with Bathsheeba and the murder of Urriah the Hittite in 2 Sam. 12:1–10.

8. See 1 Sam. 16:7.

9. Ps. 51:1 NIV; Ps. 51:10.

10. Dallas Willard, *The Divine Conspiracy: Rediscovering Our Hidden Life in God* (New York: HarperCollins, 1998), 144.

11. The word Paul uses here is similar to the English word *metamorphous*. It bears the idea of something changing its actual form.

12. Theologian David Wells used this beautiful phrase in a private lecture for Gordon-Conwell students.

13. Ps. 119:27–29 ESV. Martin Luther instructs those endeavoring to study theology to practice *oratio* (prayer), *meditatio* (meditation), and *tentatio* (trials). We can all benefit from Luther's guidance as we pursue spiritual renewal, especially utilizing prayer and meditation (or reflection). See "Preface to the Wittenberg Edition of Luther's German Writings (1539)."

14. John 10:30 ESV.

15. 1 Peter 1:22 NIV.

16. James 5:16.

17. Jer. 1:5 ESV.

18. Rom. 11:36 ESV.

19. Rom. 1:21–23.

20. These notes were taken from "The Luther Project," a private study given by Timothy Keller.

21. Gilbert K. Chesterton, *Heretics/Orthodoxy* (Nashville: Thomas Nelson, 2000), 217–18.

22. Ibid.

23. Ps. 9:10 NIV.

24. Matt. 6:26–30.

25. Heb. 10:24; Eph. 4:11–14.

26. Eugene Peterson, *The Jesus Way* (Grand Rapids, Mich.: Eerdmans, 2007), 5.

27. Michael Green, *Evangelism in the Early Church* (Grand Rapids, Mich.: Eerdmans, 2004).

28. Philip Jacob Spener, *Pia Desideria*, trans. and ed. Theodore G. Tappert (Minnesota: Fortress, 1964), 87.

29. John 16:1–6.

30. John 14:26 ASV. In this passage, Jesus promised the Holy Spirit to the disciples not only as a comforter but also as one who would help them recall the truth that Jesus taught them.

31. Pastor Philip Brooks, quoted in Wayne Jacobsen, *He Loves Me* (Newbury Park, Calif.: Windblown Media, 2007), 33.

32. "All I have needed Thy hand hath provided." From Thomas O. Chisolm, "Great Is Thy Faithfulness."

33. The thoughts here are taken from two fantastic little books by Henri Nouwen: *Here*

and Now: Living in the Spirit (New York: Crossroad, 1994), 108–10, and *Life of the Beloved: Spiritual Living in a Secular World* (New York: Crossroad, 1992), 110.

34. Nouwen, *Life of the Beloved*, 62.

35. 1 Tim. 6:7 NIV.

36. Jim Lahey with Rick Flaste, *My Bread: The Revolutionary No-Work, No-Knead Method* (New York: Norton, 2009), 20.

37. This idea of skewed relationships is based on the writings of Martin Buber, Alistair McFadyen, and Craig Gay.

38. Richard J. Foster, *Streams of Living Water: Essential Practices from the Six Great Traditions of Christian Faith* (San Francisco: HarperSanFrancisco, 2001), 177. Foster is speaking of the need for humans to participate in social justice, but the view of humanity is fitting regardless of the topic.

39. The examples of marriage and business are adapted from Bonhoeffer's *The Cost of Discipleship* and are extensions of his commentary on the word *extraordinary*. Dietrich Bonhoeffer, *The Cost of Discipleship* (New York: Touchstone, 1995), 302–3.

40. Gal. 5:22–23.

41. In Ephesus, when Christians appeared in court and were asked to state their nationality (since the city was so cosmopolitan), they would answer with "Christian." The locals, then, referred to them as "the Third Race." Inherent in the early church was their diversity. Christianity did not recognize distinction in race or status. It leveled the playing field. This was a huge draw since so much emphasis was put on socioeconomic status, master-slave relationship, and Jews versus Greeks. Christianity was a kind of filter for humanity, the antithesis to the confusion and separation of Babel.

42. Cyril Richardson, *Early Christian Fathers* (New York: Simon and Schuster, 1996), 217.

43. Ibid.

44. C. S. Lewis, *Miracles* (New York: Macmillan, 1960), 111–12.

45. Richardson, *Early Christian Fathers*, 217. This letter stems from a document known as "The So-Called Letter to Diognetus: The Mystery of the New People." Diognetus was an emperor. This letter is believed to be Asian in its origin, written around the second or third century during the persecutions. There are scholarly disagreements regarding the authorship of the letter, so the common understanding rests with anonymity. Though there is some mystery surrounding the document, the heavy theological overtones cannot be mistaken. Strands of the apostle Paul's thought are evident, as are John's and Peter's. Regardless of its mystery, the letter holds some of the most beautiful language describing the early Christians.

46. See Luke 24:32 ESV.

Postlude

1. Henry Wadsworth Longfellow, *The Spanish Student* (Boston: Houghton, Mifflin Co., 1881), 49.

Authors' Note

1. See *http://www.mediadecay.com/2010/03/great-concerts-pearl-jam/*.